SCOTTISH FOOTBALL QUOTATIONS

Kenny MacDonald has been a full-time journalist since 1977, covering club and international football at home and abroad. Since 1991 he has worked for the *News of the World* in Glasgow. As an impartial professional, he shows the red card to personal feelings when he reaches for his pencil and notebook, and can be relied upon for fearless but fair appraisals of Scottish football. However, he admits his favourite colours are claret and amber, and his professional highlight was reporting on the 1991 Scottish Cup final. He is married and lives in Glasgow.

SCOTTISH

FOOTBALL

QUOTATIONS

KENNY MACDONALD

MAINSTREAM
PUBLISHING
EDINBURGH AND LONDON

For Jacquie, Jack, and Ben.
And for Steve Kirk.

First published in Great Britain in 1994 by
MAINSTREAM PUBLISHING COMPANY (EDINBURGH) LTD
7 Albany Street
Edinburgh EH1 3UG

ISBN 1 85158 643 1

A catalogue record for this book is available from the
British Library

Typeset in Palatino by CentraCet Ltd, Cambridge
Printed and bound in Great Britain by
Biddles Ltd, Guildford and King's Lynn

CONTENTS

ACKNOWLEDGMENTS

Thanks:
Doug Baillie, Bill Bateson, Alan Dick, Jim Duffy, Tom English, Brian Fair, Ray Farningham, Roddy Forsyth, Martin Frizell, John Gahagan, Donald Hallam, Stephen Hope, Davie Irons, Hugh Keevins, Kevin McCarra, Ally McCoist, K. C. MacDonald, Archie MacGregor, Jim McInally, Alastair McSporran, Stuart Rafferty, Tommy Reilly, Ian Ross, Phil Shaw, Scott Struthers, Jason Tomas, David Walker.

Hello:
My mother and father, David Ackles, Johnnie Allan, Tim Allan, Gary Armitage, Gwen Armstrong, David Belcher, Jim Black, Allan Bryce, Eric Carroll, Agnes Cassells, Liesha Clark, Stuart Cosgrove, Ronnie Cully, Gordon Dryden, Wild Man Fischer, Jan-Erik Fjeld, Ronnie Gurr, Ross Jack, Gary Keown, Graeme Kerr, Miodrag Krivokapic, Gary Larson, David Leslie, Colin McAdam, Gary McAllister, Maureen McCarroll, Deborah MacClare, Alan McCusker-Thompson, Lindsay MacDonald, Alexandra McKain, Stevie McKenzie, Joe McLaughlin, Alex McLeish, Terry McMahon, Lynne McMillan, Steven McNeil, Alan Mackin, Danny Marlin, Michael Marra, Ally Maxwell, Campbell Money, Bert Muirhead, Iain Munro, Neil Murray, Eric Musgrave, Pat Nevin, Ron Newey, Charlie Nicholas, Claire Oldfield, John Peel, Susan Purdie, Joyce Sawkins, Brian Scott, Neil Scott, Simon Stainrod, Gregor Stevens, Geoff Thompson, Loudon Wainwright III, Jordana Welles, Steve Welsh, Ian Wood.

THE PAST

Then strip lads and to it, though sharp be the weather,
And if, by mischance, you should happen to fall,
There are worse things in life than a tumble in the heather,
And life itself is but a game of football.
Sir Walter Scott, on a match between Ettrick and Selkirk, 1815.

TIES IN THE NORTHERN DICTRICT: The clubs in this district connected with the SFA played off their ties in the first round for the national trophy on Saturday and some phenomenal scoring was witnessed. At Gayfield, Arbroath, the Arbroath beat the Bon Accord, Aberdeen, by 36 goals to none; while in East Dock Street Park, Dundee, the Harp defeated the Aberdeen Rovers by 35 goals to nil.
The unflappable **Glasgow Herald** displays considerable *sang-froid* as it brings news of the game's biggest score, 14 September 1885.

Association Football is becoming notorious for scenes and disgraceful exhibitions of ruffianism. The rabble will soon make it impossible for law-abiding citizens to attend matches.
Scottish Athletic Journal, 1887.

Before the game had finished the moon had risen and amid its quivering beams the match picturesquely closed.
Motherwell Standard report on Motherwell v Celtic match, 20 April 1916.
Both sides had played in the afternoon and this match kicked off at 6.30 p.m.
During wartime football was played only on Saturdays and holidays.

The Raith Rovers party – a mere 13 players plus manager and directors – set off for the Canary Isles in May 1923. It seemed they were more in search of sun and fun than strenuous opposition, with a stop-off at Vigo in Spain to watch a bullfight as part of the itinerary. Indeed, the trip might have remained no more than a footnote in the club's history had the ship carrying the team not run aground on the rocks off the Spanish coast.
John Harding, *Alex James: Life of a Football Legend*, 1988.

Pray for rain.
Skipper **Jimmy McMullan**'s advice to Scotland players before the Wembley international of 1928. Only Alex Jackson stood over 5' 6". It rained and Scotland won 5–1.

Most of the players were top pros from England, Scotland and Ireland and I benefited from their experiences, especially when we played against the Glasgow Rangers in 1928. They are still the greatest team I ever saw . . . the Rangers manager asked me to go back to Scotland with them, but the World Cup was on my young mind and I was making more than the Rangers were paying anyway.
America's 'Best Player Ever', **Bill Gonsalves**, on an early Ibrox signing bid.

A hair-raising individual performance by Auld and a pass to Brown gave us our lone score.
Extract from report by **Wilfred Cummings**, manager of the USA national side in the 1930 World Cup, on the semi-final defeat by Argentina. Goalscorer James Brown and Andrew Auld were among five Scots players in the US side, who were also coached and trained by Scots. Brown, who emigrated as a teenager, is the only Scot – so far – to score in the semi-finals of the World Cup.

At the height of the Depression in 1933, Hampden admitted 134,710 spectators without the benefit of tickets to witness Scotland's 2–1 defeat of England. Two years later the official attendance at the same fixture had fallen to 126,693 but there were scenes of dangerous chaos outside the ground and it was thought likely that over 200,000 fans had crammed themselves into the stadium. When tickets were introduced for the 1937 Scotland v England international, 150,000 briefs were sold although 453 ticket-holders apparently failed to make it through the turnstiles because the official crowd figure is recorded as 149,547 . . . The fanatical devotion to football in the West of Scotland at that time is further emphasised by the fact that on the Saturday afterwards 146,433 paid to watch Celtic and Aberdeen contest the 1937 Scottish Cup final at the same venue.
Roddy Forsyth, *The Only Game*, 1990.

The ground of Larbert Amateurs, who were to play Morton in the second round of the [1938] Cup, was found on closer

inspection by the representatives of the SFA to have a bricked-up boundary wall which prevented the ball from going out for a corner at one junction.
Hugh Keevins and **Kevin McCarra**, *100 Cups: The Story of the Scottish Cup.*

I was getting changed one day and suddenly I saw the spats appear. That was Mr Struth, always very smartly dressed. He said, 'How much do I pay you a week, boy?' I was 16 at the time and I said, 'A pound a week, sir.' He said, 'Any boy that can keep these boots as polished as that deserves more than a pound a week. From now you'll get two pounds a week.' I hadn't the heart to tell him my mother cleaned my boots.
Willie Thornton, *Only a Game?*, BBC documentary, 1985.

We ain't got a chance against your boys. But we're gonna fight hard to keep down a cricket score.
America's Scottish coach **Bill Jeffrey**, before beating England in the 1950 World Cup in Brazil. Jeffrey was from Edinburgh and emigrated when he was 20. The Americans were also captained by a Scot, Eddie McIlvenny.

There was talk of a movie script, with Sean Connery playing Bill Jeffrey. It was to be a *Chariots of Fire* type of thing – a crowd of working men against the full-time English players. But I don't know what became of it.
Walter Bahr, who played for the American team which beat England 1–0 in the 1950 World Cup, on plans to celebrate the result.

It was on the Monday before the Scotland v Hungary match in December 1954. I was in Marks & Spencer in Sauchiehall Street and I noticed a man at the next counter having trouble making himself understood. I thought he was a Polish seaman and I asked in Polish if I could help. He shook his head and said, 'Not Polish – Hungarian.' He said his name was Puskas . . . He asked what Scottish footballers were paid and was very surprised when I said some of the big clubs paid £15 a week. He told me he was a Roman Catholic and I spoke to him about Celtic. He was very interested. Then he burst out, 'I am sick of this Hungarian football. For three months we lived in a camp, training. Always the Hungarians must be the best. No one can beat us.' He was not happy and he was afraid if he failed at football he might be put back in the Hungarian Army. He

really became interested in staying in Scotland after the rest of the Hungarians left after the match.
Polish-born **Czeslaw Muchniewski**, *Sunday Mail*, 28 October 1956. The story ran under the headline, 'PUSKAS TRIED TO FLEE TO SCOTLAND'. Puskas had been reported dead in the Hungarian uprising.

Many years ago I watched Gordon Smith running up the wing keeping the ball up on his head. It was a credit to Third Lanark, who didn't hack him down. I've only ever seen it once in my life. The old supporters talk about it yet.
Hibs striker **Lawrie Reilly**, *Ony a Game?*, BBC documentary, 1985.

The scenes outside the ground, when I arrived early, were quite unbelievable. The whole of the carpark, from Aikenhead Road to Cathcart Road, was black with people. There must have been at least 50,000 people, in orderly queues, no violence, no rushing – everything was correct – and by about four o'clock in the afternoon we had sold 134,000 tickets.
Former SFA secretary **Ernie Walker** on the 1960 European Cup final between Real Madrid and Eintracht Frankfurt. Walker was in charge of ticket sales.

The last time a team in Scotland lived up to the fans' expectations was in 1960 when Real Madrid beat Eintracht in Glasgow.
Scotland coach **Andy Roxburgh**, November 1986.

The trouble that day was that they used an orange ball. Eric Caldow and I were afraid to kick it and Billy McNeill was afraid to touch it.
Rangers defender **Bobby Shearer** on Scotland's 9–3 defeat by England, 1961.

Slim Jim had everything required of a great Scottish footballer. Outrageously skilled, totally irresponsible, supremely arrogant and thick as mince.
Alastair McSporran, *The Absolute Game* fanzine, 1990.

Nae wonder they call him the Galloping Major. I understand it now.
Jim Baxter, after taking Ferenc Puskas to a party in Drumchapel following the Rangers v Real Madrid European Cup tie, 25 September 1963. It was alleged Puskas had made a brand new friend among the affair's female guests.

One day Davie Wilson accidentally caught Pat Crerand with his elbow in the teeth. And Paddy was always very proud of his teeth. I remember Paddy saying to him, 'It's all right Davie, unless I've got to lose it. If I've got to lose it, you're going to suffer.'
Billy McNeill, *Only a Game?*, BBC documentary, 1985.

When I joined Rangers I immediately established myself as third-choice left-half. The guys ahead of me were an amputee and a Catholic.
Scotland boss **Craig Brown** recalling his glittering Ibrox career, 1990s.

It was a Friday and we were playing Rangers the next day so we had a five-a-side match to get some practice. Wee Jimmy came along and joined in and we couldn't get the ball off him for 20 minutes. We all stopped and I was looking at Davie Provan and Frank McGarvey and Danny McGrain and thinking, this isn't supposed to be happening because we're practising for a big game. He was there for 20 minutes with the ball, sitting on it, doing everything with it. I've never seen an exhibition like it. Unbelievable, he was.
Charlie Nicholas on Jimmy Johnstone.

Before we played Italy at Hampden in the World Cup in 1965, Jim (Baxter) was prancing up and down the dressing-room saying, 'Rivera? I'll Rivera him when I get out there.'
Billy Bremner on Gianni Rivera, the top Italian player of his generation, *Only a Game?*, BBC documentary, 1985.

A man appeared at the door and started to tell me about Rangers Football Club and even laid a form on the table for me to sign. Being from Edinburgh and being from a household that supported Hearts I didn't want to sign the form, but in those days you did what your father told you, and my father said 'Sign'. . . When the man walked out with my signature on the registration form I remember starting to cry at 16 years of age. I remember saying to my father, 'You've made me sign for a team I don't want to play for.' But I watched Rangers – for the first time, I may add – the following Saturday against Hibs at Easter Road. Rangers won 6–1 and I remember turning to my pal and saying, 'This is some team I've signed for.'
John Greig, 1993, *Glasgow Rangers Revisited: A 120–Year History*.

If you were looking for a replica of Bill Struth, Willie Waddell was the nearest you could get to him.
John Greig, 1993.

I've always believed in treating the ball like a woman. Give it a cuddle, caress it a wee bit, take your time, and you'll get the required response.
Jim Baxter, 1991.

In my time under big Jock Stein you had to come back every afternoon and work overtime, not even to get on the bench but just to get a seat on the bus to go and see the first team play.
Celtic boss **Lou Macari**, November 1993.

1967 AND ALL THAT . . .

We don't just want to win this cup. We want to win by playing
good football, to make neutrals glad we won it.
Jock Stein before the 1967 European Cup final.

[I was] not so much drifting as rushing headlong out of the
game. By then [1964] I was 33, and frankly I wasn't too
bothered whether I played again or not, because I'd had a
good career. I was working as a rep for an oil company, and
enjoying my golf. I was still getting about seven pounds a
week from Hibs, and the only time I went there was to pick up
my wage . . . A friend of mine, Ian Spence, who was manager
of Berwick Rangers, came and asked me if I'd play for them. I
told him I wasn't interested in playing any more, but while he
was there I got a phone call from Jock [Stein, then Hibs boss].
He told me to come down to the ground immediately. When I
got there he said Sean Fallon of Celtic had rung to ask if I
wanted to go to Parkhead. It seemed ridiculous. I hadn't
kicked a ball for months, and this man wanted me to sign for
Celtic.
Ronnie Simpson, *The European Cup, 1955–1980.*

The night before the game England played Spain at Wembley
and it was on TV. Big Jock knew this lad called Lennox who
had a business in Estoril. We were all invited to his home to
watch the international and I remember walking back, walking
along the road and through little bits of wood and the whole
thing was totally carefree and casual. It helped relax us and
settle us. He'd already done the preparations. He'd told us we
had to stay out of the sun for a couple of days before it. It
wasn't a holiday. We were there to do a job.
Billy McNeill, *Only a Game?*, BBC documentary, 1985.

In Lisbon I saw the manager pounce on a player sitting in the
Palacio Hotel in Estoril simply because he had his head
exposed to the sun coming through the window. And that was
his reserve goalkeeper!
Archie MacPherson, *Action Replays*, 1991.

Every time we opened a cupboard a Celtic supporter fell out.
British consulate officials on the 12,000 Celtic fans who made it to Lisbon,
The European Cup, 1955–1980.

When we went on to the field we found Herrera had sent out some of his men to claim our bench. I had my trainers with me and we just pushed them out of the way. We won that one and in a sense that went a long way towards winning the match.
Jock Stein, *The European Cup, 1955–1980*.

All he said before we went into the tunnel was, 'I'm proud of you for getting this far. You've made history. Go out and play as you're capable of playing.'
Bertie Auld, *Only a Game?*, BBC documentary, 1985.

Suddenly a man came looming out of the darkness towards us. I couldn't believe it. It was a bloke called McConville that I knew from Chapelhall. Heaven knows how he'd done it but he'd got past all the security at the biggest match in Europe to come and look for the team.
Celtic's **John Clark**'s memories of the tunnel in Lisbon, 1967.

I suppose the contrast must have been funny. They were sleek and tanned like film stars. On our side there were quite a few with no teeth and we had blobs of vaseline on our eyebrows to block out the sweat
Bobby Murdoch.

How could you feel nervous? You looked at the ability there was in every man around you, from old man Simpson in goal out to wee Bobby at number 11. Whatever happened, Celtic had the ability to handle it.
Bertie Auld.

I gave Ronnie [Simpson] my set of false teeth to put in the back of the net with his own. I did that because I thought there would be photographers all round us after we'd won and I didn't want them to get pictures of me flashing a pair of gums at them.
Bobby Lennox.

We'd seen films of Inter and we knew all the great international stars in their side. I don't believe any of us thought we had a chance at all. We thought we were on a drubbing. We were going around trying to gee each other up, saying that we would make the most of the day no matter what.
Jimmy Johnstone.

When we came out of the dressing-room for the second-half [a goal down], some of the lads were singing, which must have astonished the Italians.
John Clark, *The European Cup, 1955–1980.*

As I came to shoot a defender stopped and half-turned his back on me. If he'd taken another step it would have been very difficult for me to get the ball past him. They say the book of Italian heroes is very thin and he wasn't interested in expanding it any!
Tommy Gemmell on the equaliser.

If the Inter defender had blocked the ball and Inter had gone up and scored I was the one who'd have got the bollocking because I shouldn't have been up there when Jim Craig was up there.
Tommy Gemmell, *Only a Game?*, BBC documentary, 1985.

It was the shot Gemmell had been born to hit.
Kevin McCarra and **Pat Woods**, *One Afternoon in Lisbon.*

Before we left Parkhead for Lisbon he had us run through this tactic time and time again, almost as if he knew it would pay off in that particular game.
Steve Chalmers on the winning goal.

There wasn't a team in the world who could've played defensive football against the Celtic team of that time and not lose matches.
Tommy Gemmell, *Only a Game?*, BBC documentary, 1985.

Many times I tried to get forward in the match, but when I played the ball and ran, I did not get it back. Really, we were five men against 11.
Inter full-back **Giacinto Facchetti**, *The European Cup, 1955–1980.*

I cannot remember Inter Milan winning one corner-kick, and as far as I can recollect I think I had only two goal-kicks throughout the match. According to one statistician Celtic had two shots which hit wood, 13 which were saved, 17 blocked or deflected and 19 wide or high. I only remember holding one weak shot and I certainly didn't concede a corner-kick. On reflection, it was just about my easiest game of the season.

Ronnie Simpson, *Sure it's a Grand Old Team to Play For.*

While all around was complete bedlam, I noticed the boss was seated, totally unmoved by the whole shindig. Then it dawned. Jock Stein had such complete faith in his players that he expected to win the European Cup.

Ronnie Simpson, August 1978.

On his [Stein's] face was not the slightest indication of triumph or satisfaction. Indeed, he looked angry. He was trying to push supporters away with a ferocity that would have been the envy of a nightclub bouncer . . . I recall him throwing one supporter off his feet with a mighty sweep of his arm.

Archie MacPherson on the aftermath, *Action Replays*, 1991.

We can have no complaints. Celtic deserve their victory. We were beaten by their force. Although we lost, the match was a victory for sport.

Inter coach **Helenio Herrera**.

Words just cannot express this achievement after such a wonderful season. This is a fitting climax.

Rangers boss **Scot Symon**.

It was inevitable: sooner or later, the Inter of Herrera, the Inter of *catenaccio*, of negative football, of marginal victories, had to pay for their refusal to play entertaining football.

Lisbon newspaper ***Mundo Desportivo***, 1967.

I went into the dressing-room after the game and he'd just come out of the bath. He was sweating as much as the players and I said to him, 'Jock, you're immortal now.'

Liverpool boss **Bill Shankly**, *Only a Game?*, BBC documentary, 1985.

1972

It's only recently I've got a full video of that game, and when I watch it I think what a terrible match it was.

Captain **John Greig** on Rangers' European Cup-Winners' Cup victory over Dynamo Moscow in Barcelona, May 1972, *Only a Game?*, BBC documentary, 1985.

I'd been out for about six weeks with a bad ankle and quite honestly I shouldn't have played. I wasn't fit.

John Greig on 1972, *Only a Game?*, BBC documentary, 1985.

It was one of the biggest disappointments of my life. To have achieved what we did that night was lost. We were handed the cup in a small room and more or less told, 'Get out our road'.

John Greig on Barcelona.

It's a tender spot in my life, because you just live to parade cups. The police's authority was being questioned and they did what they were trained to do and charged, and the Rangers fans did what they were apt to do, they charged. It upset me terribly and it upset the players that they couldn't show the world this cup they'd won.

Jock Wallace, *Only a Game?*, BBC documentary, 1985.

I don't think half the Rangers supporters saw that cup.

John Greig, *Only a Game?*, BBC documentary, 1985.

It would not have taken too much re-organising to have brought the Rangers captain to the middle of the stand and presented the cup there . . . The crowd, having come all this way, felt entitled to public acclamation of the triumph. The authorities tried to cap the gusher. If the supporters had simply been allowed to protest vocally, or carouse on the pitch, Barcelona would have been forgotten by the following week. Disastrously, the police decided to act.

Archie MacPherson on Barcelona 1972, *Action Replays*, 1991.

Will they take the cup off us?
Reaction of Rangers reserve **Alex Miller**, reading news reports of the Barcelona riot after the Cup-Winners' Cup win 1972, quoted in Archie MacPherson, *Action Replays*, 1991.

The emphasis was being placed naturally enough on the conduct of the Rangers supporters. In other words, on the aftermath of the assault by the police. The riot was not fully described. Scandalously, it never officially was. When we made efforts to try to rationalise and apportion blame fairly we were condemned by the public. There was one special reason for that. We had not shown the riot. Letters and phone calls poured in on us. We were accused of hiding the truth, of toadying to 'that' club, of being cowardly.
Archie MacPherson on Barcelona 1972, *Action Replays*, 1991. The Spanish TV director had ordered cameras not to film the fighting.

1974

My neighbour is Hugh Taylor, the football correspondent of the *Daily Record*. He was nattering down telephone lines about this, the greatest game of all, long before I was born. His hands go round my neck, hot, wet tears drench my jumper, and he weeps. So do I.

Ian Archer, *Glasgow Herald*, June 1974, after the 1–1 draw with Yugoslavia. Scotland went out of the World Cup on goal difference following this match.

Willie Ormond came into our dressing-room afterwards and congratulated us. Nothing finer will happen in the tournament.

Yugoslav boss **Miljan Miljanic** after the same game.

1978

Retain it!
Ally MacLeod, on being asked what he planned to do after the World Cup, 1978.

I didn't fancy it. It was terrible. I can look back and laugh now but I didn't like it at the time.
Ally MacLeod on the Hampden send-off to Argentina, *Only a Game?*, BBC documentary, 1985.

At first the plan was for the entire squad to be introduced to the crowd on the park and then to soar away in a helicopter for a big finish. It was only when the astronomical cost of insuring players for that piece of aeronautical theatrics was realised, to say nothing of the safety aspect for the crowd below, that the idea was abbreviated to the ceremony on the pitch.
Danny McGrain, *In Sunshine or in Shadow*, 1987.

We were even ready for the trivia which would catch some other teams out, like the razor-sharp toilet-paper which could easily leave you with two bums if you're not careful.
Willie Johnston, *On the Wing!*

I told him several of our players smoked and it would be untruthful to back an anti-smoking campaign.
Ally MacLeod to Dr David Player, head of the Scottish Health Education unit, over calls for Scotland to reject sponsorship money from the British American Tobacco Company, 1978.

If clever people had been in charge, they would have taken the pressure off us by telling us we were coming to play the best players in the world. Instead we were bombarded with crap about beating the rest of the world into the ground. How could anyone be so optimistic about our chances? When did you last see Scotland play really good football, play with positive rhythm and a consistent pattern?
Lou Macari on Argentina 1978. (Quoted in *World Cup* by David Miller.)

Tunisia and Iran are better prepared than we are. In our last match before coming here the lads exhausted themselves trying to beat England. It couldn't be any other way with 80,000 mad Scotsmen yelling 'Gie us an English heid!'
Lou Macari, 1978.

Willie's my best mate, so when he tries to kick my head off you can tell how well things are going.
Martin Buchan, who needed stitches after being accidentally kicked in the face by Willie Donachie against Iran, before the Holland game, Argentina 1978. (Quoted in *The Story of Football.*)

Once England's hopes of competing in the World Cup had vanished, it was an understandable case of transferred nationalism that the English, instantly restyling themselves the British, should heap Scotland with the burden of national expectations. But it was hubris to be so confident that Scotland would do well. Television, during the past week, has not been as bad as the press in pouring scorn on Ally and his army, but it was at least as bad in the way it built them up in the first place. The best you can say in mitigation is that the Scots themselves showed less judgment than anybody.
Clive James, *The Observer*, June 1978.

It isn't the likes of Argentina or West Germany that worry me. You have to motivate Scottish players for games against teams like Peru and Iran where we think we've got the game won before we start. They worry me a lot more than Holland.
Ally MacLeod before the World Cup.

The tune began changing when the Peruvians, one goal down, suddenly revealed an ability to run faster with the ball than the Scots could run without it.
Clive James, *The Observer*, June 1978.

Peru want two things in a game. They want to play one-twos going into the penalty area and they want to win free-kicks just outside. In that position, to South Americans, a free-kick is as good as a penalty.
Bobby Charlton, 1978.

Everybody said we shouldn't bother going to Argentina. We were under no pressure. Of everything that happened, I remember the free-kick most. When I saw the wall, I saw one space. The moment I saw the goalie prepare the wall, I thought, 'There's no way he is going to stop this.' It was a big mistake by the goalie, a big mistake.
Two-goal Peru striker **Teofilo Cubillas** remembers 1978.

Two days of recriminations followed, exacerbated by Willie Johnston's little blunder with the pills. Willie flew home to be dressed down by Frank Bough. 'You shouldn't be here at all, should you? You should be out there playing World Cup football for Scotland. How do you feel?'
Clive James, *The Observer*, June 1978.

I had problems of my own before the [Peru] game, as I was feeling lousy with a stuffed-up nose and a slight chestiness. I put it down to another bout of hay-fever, to which I am prone . . . Over an hour before the kick-off I confirmed the time with Sandy Jardine and proceeded to take two of the pills, quite openly, in a last effort to clear the stuffiness.
Willie Johnston, *On the Wing!*

After the game, myself and Kenny Dalglish went in. I remember looking into the jar and mine's was a terrible colour, it was the colour of lager. I'm thinking, 'Doesn't look too clever, that.' I went back on the bus to our camp and the next morning Ally sent for me. He said, 'Your dope test is positive, what did you take?' I said I took two tablets and that was the start of it.
Willie Johnston, *Only a Game?*, BBC documentary, 1985.

Many of the lads were shocked when they discovered the Reactivan pills were to blame, because some of them had used them before at home, just as I had. They were very common items in England, obtainable by free access from any doctor, and some of the boys must have been thankful that they weren't taking them to shake off an injury.
Willie Johnston, *On the Wing!*

There was no way I deliberately and knowingly took drugs. I never realised for a minute that those pills contained anything strong enough to even stimulate me into opening my eyes in

the morning, let alone dope me up for a hectic 90 minutes of World Cup football . . . No doubt I was guilty of something, probably ignorance more than anything else . . . but I was dumbfounded by the accusation that I had deliberately cheated by taking drugs.
Willie Johnston, *On the Wing!*

Willie Johnston was someone I had disliked playing against when he was with Rangers. I did not know him personally but I could see that on the park his mouth was never shut and he was a perpetually gesticulating bundle of nervous energy . . . Once we had come together for Scotland, though, I found him to be pleasant, approachable and a very down-to-earth man. He was almost shy, in fact, and his nervous streak always gave itself away when he was violently ill before very big international . . . I could not believe, and to this day I still cannot accept, that he knowingly did anything wrong.
Danny McGrain, *In Sunshine or in Shadow*, 1987.

When my mum tuned into the news, the first thing she saw was a picture of me staring back at her. Her immediate reaction was, 'Oh no, it's oor Billy. He's dead. They've shot him!'
Willie Johnston, *On the Wing!*

When we got hold of the tablets, the Celtic doctor said, 'We better just throw them away.' We were passing this field which was full of Argentinian cows and we threw the pills in the field. When we came back from training that day, the cows were all jumping around all over the place. They think I made that story up, but that's a true story.
Ally MacLeod, *Only a Game?*, BBC documentary, 1985.

He [Willie Johnston] was just your typical average Scottish bampot ball-player whose loyalties were torn between the Scottish national team and Scottish & Newcastle Breweries.
Only an Excuse '93 stage show.

I want to congratulate Scotland for the team they presented to us.
Peru manager **Marcus Calderon**, after the game.

You can say it's been an education to us.
Tunisian coach **Abdel Majid Chetali**, 1978. The Tunisians shared Scotland's training camp.

Scotland would need to win by a lot of goals [against Iran] if they were going to qualify. Some darker voices suggested they might only win by a few goals. Only the known Cassandras – mad creatures with rent garments and tresses in disarray – dared to speculate that Scotland might not win at all.
Clive James, *The Observer*, June 1978. The final score was 1–1.

We sold all these copies and the day after Iran drew with Scotland a guy in Dundee was selling it for a penny and giving you a hammer to break it with. I put all the money I made from the single into an LP, financed it myself, and it was released the day after we drew with Iran. There's about 30,000 lying in a garage up in Clarkston somewhere.
Comedian **Andy Cameron** on his 1978 hit record, 'Ally's Army', *Only a Game?*, BBC documentary, 1985.

Gemmill . . . good play by Gemmill, and again . . . 3–1! A brilliant individual goal by this hard little professional has put Scotland in dreamland.
Commentator **David Coleman** records Archie Gemmill's goal against Holland in Mendoza, 11 June 1978.

If we had qualified for the next round there could have been even more shame heaped on Scotland as certain players had decided they were heading home whatever the result either because of flak from their families over the fabricated tales or because the knew they were out of the team reckoning.
Graeme Souness on the aftermath of the Holland game, *No Half Measures*, 1985.

Mr Dennis Canavan: As the recent incident involving the use of drugs in Argentina brought Scottish football into even more disrepute than the team's pathetic performance on the field, does my Honourable Friend agree that it is now up to the SFA . . . to try and restore Scotland's good name by insisting on the highest standards and if necessary the use of spot checks to enforce these regulations?
Mr Frank McElhone: I agree . . . indeed, FIFA has asked the

FA and the SFA to conduct inquiries into drug-taking in football.

Mr Norman Buchan: Will the minister tell us whether there is any truth in the rumour that stimulants were used by the journalists and tranquillisers by the players?

Mr Frank McElhone: The only good thing that came out of the whole exercise was that my Right Honourable friend went to see Scotland play Holland. I think his magnetic influence on the play brought about the good result. We are all sorry he did not go to the first two games.

Extract from **Hansard**, 1977–78, Volume 952, 21 June 1978.

Derek Johnstone and I went to Argentina. Neither of us got a game but at least they were singing my song.

Comedian **Andy Cameron**.

a) The player Don Masson, having admitted to the Office Bearers that he had given false information to the Association's Team Manager and Medical Officer on a most important issue in Argentina, and having expressed the view publicly that he would prefer not to play for Scotland, should be accommodated in his desire.

b) The Team Manager, when selecting players in future, should be recommended to bear in mind the vehement complaints against the Association and its arrangements publicly expressed by the player, Lou Macari, and should give serious consideration to the advisability of subjecting the player again to these arrangements, which he professes to find so unsatisfactory.

Extract from **SFA minutes**, 10 July 1978.

We just had to skulk around and not talk to English people. Everybody in this country was reduced by what happened over there.

Journalist **Ian Archer**, *Only a Game?*, BBC documentary, 1985.

That was possibly the finest 18 months Scottish fans have ever had. We maybe didn't win the World Cup, but we had a wonderful 18 months.

Ally MacLeod, *Only a Game?*, BBC documentary, 1985.

1982

I spent most of time in Sotogrande sitting in a darkened room on my own. I cannot take the sun and Jock Stein was so determined that I would not suffer one bit from heat stroke that he went around the place watching me like a hawk. Any time I stayed out for more than twenty minutes or so the Big Man would be there ordering me indoors. The most exciting thing that would happen after that was when Willie Miller came into the room after his spell in the sun. Then, instead of sitting there with nothing to do. I could sit and watch Willie sleeping. That was a high spot of the afternoon.

Gordon Strachan on the Spain World Cup, *Strachan Style*, 1991.

The last two goals were scored in a drawn game with Russia that was a demonstration of the melodrama we take on tour every four years. Scotland takes the lead. Scotland loses the lead with a goal that would cause a fight among schoolboys on Glasgow Green. Scotland equalises late on but goes out of the competition by the narrowest of margins.

Danny McGrain on 1982, *In Sunshine or in Shadow*, 1987.

Jock Stein, to his eternal shame, persisted in fielding [Alan] Hansen alongside Willie Miller, when it was patently obvious that neither of them were prepared to shoulder the responsibility of attacking the ball – except, of course, for that farcical, trouser-moistening moment in Malaga when they attempted to do so simultaneously.

Gary Oliver, *The Absolute Game* fanzine, November 1993.

1983

We had begun to think we would win the Cup-Winners' Cup after we beat Bayern in the quarter-finals. [German] teams had done us a lot of damage in European competitions so when we put Bayern out we began to think we could go all the way.
Willie Miller.

Gothenburg convinced us we were a good side. That started in the tunnel before the match when Alex Ferguson said, 'Get out there and let's hear you shout!' We shouted a bit in the tunnel and a couple of Real Madrid players shouted back in imitation of us as a bit of a joke, but you could see they were just a bit apprehensive.
Alex McLeish, 1990.

I put on John Hewitt for the injured Eric Black and then very nearly substituted Andy Watson for Hewitt to give us more pace in the middle of the park.
Alex Ferguson on Gothenburg, *A Light in the North*, 1985.

They [Real] were given a free-kick from a scoring position when we already made it time-up. They took it before the referee blew and it was ordered to be retaken. Just prior to that second free-kick, big Bryan Gunn, our reserve goalkeeper who was sitting beside me on the bench, got down on his knees and said, 'Dear God, please let them miss it.' I loved him for that. The ball whistled past and the referee blew for full-time.
Alex Ferguson, *A Light in the North*, 1985.

When the ref blew the whistle I remember getting off the bench, we all sprang up, and I slipped. And all the staff ran over the top of me.
Alex Ferguson on Gothenburg, *Only a Game?*, BBC documentary, 1985.

I even brought whisky for Di Stefano, the Real Madrid manager. He appreciated it.
Alex Ferguson on the success against Real, 1983, *A Light in the North*.

1986

Alan Hansen was so nice about it when I talked to him, I felt like a slug. In fact, lower than a snake.
Alex Ferguson tells Hansen he isn't going to Mexico, May 1986.

I was playing perhaps the best football of my career. I could understand being omitted from the 11 in the team but not from the 22 in the squad. I got on with Alex then and I get on with him now, but I have never understood it.
Alan Hansen on Alex Ferguson's decision to leave him out of Scotland's 1986 World Cup squad, April 1993.

From Hansen's comments, you would imagine that he had been a mainstay whose axing was both sudden and unexpected. Nothing of the sort. With the exception of a fleeting appearance in Kenny Dalglish's 100th international – a fixture so competitive that even Roy Aitken got his name on the scoresheet – his previous outing came in 1983, would you believe, when he was pulled off at half-time with Switzerland two goals ahead and tiptoeing through the Scots defence at will.
Gary Oliver, *The Absolute Game* fanzine, October 1993.

I won't be watching. I'll take my wife out for a meal. If I looked at the games I'd go back to feeling the way I did when the manager said I wasn't going.
David Speedie learns he's not going to Mexico, May 1986.

He's the nearest thing to Kenny we have.
Scotland interim boss **Alex Ferguson**, announcing Steve Archibald would replace the injured Kenny Dalglish in Scotland's World Cup squad, May 1986.

He [Steve Archibald] has in the past been likened to an unleashed cobra, but not by anyone who's seen him play football.
It's Only an Excuse, BBC Radio Scotland spoof documentary, 1986.

The hotel was a disaster. The rooms were small and carved out of stone to give it a 'natural' effect. To me it was like living in a cave. Honestly, I felt like a bear cub waiting for someone to come along and toss me a few scraps of meat . . . we would have been better off living in tents.

Gordon Strachan on Scotland's Mexico City hotel, *Strachan Style*, 1991.

We were quite literally afraid to do anything . . . Other teams can be more sophisticated. Other teams can be better technically. Other teams can be more disciplined and more organised, but Scottish teams can still beat them. That, however, was not on the cards against the South Americans. We were too frightened to give in to our natural instincts and have a real go in the game. Not frightened of being being kicked or even of being injured. We expected that. But frightened that if we fought fire with fire there would be a riot. If just one of us retaliated then there would be one of those huge on-field brawls where anything might have happened.

Gordon Strachan on the World Cup tie against Uruguay, *Strachan Style*, 1991.

I remember thinking at one stage if you had to sink as low as this to find success in a World Cup, then it was just not worth it.

Gordon Strachan on Uruguay, *Strachan Style*, 1991.

As we drove away from the magnificent new stadium which stood out of its slum surroundings like some kind of obscenity, I found myself able to understand them [Uruguay]. Here we were passing through the kind of streets so many South American footballers grow up in. Dead dogs were lying in the road. People were living in cardboard houses. The children were in rags . . . it is the old hungry fighter thing . . . That is what the game means to them. It is their means of survival. It has given them a new life, and probably handed whole families the lifeline they would never otherwise have reached. They can take their mothers and fathers, their brothers and sisters, away from slums like Neza. They can marry and raise a family in decent surroundings and educate their children. Even feed and clothe them, because they have been born with soccer skills. That's some motivation. And sure as hell we could not match it!

Gordon Strachan, *Strachan Style*, 1991.

The referee was a murderer.
Uruguay manager **Omar Borras**, after Uruguay had José Batista sent off in the first minute of the 0–0 draw with Scotland.

I am sitting here wondering what the hell is going on. This conference is a complete shambles. I've listened to Mr Borras. He has no respect for other people's dignity. He is simply lying and cheating. If this is what happens I'm glad to be going home.
Alex Ferguson, 13 June 1986.

The TV audience of 700 million who watched the 1986 World Cup final may have been aware that the Argentinian defender with the unlikely name of John Brown, who scored the opening goal against West Germany, had a Scottish great-grandfather.
Roddy Forsyth, *The Only Game*, 1990.

1990

I was with the Costa Rica team before they played Scotland in the last World Cup. I told them, 'In 1978, everybody expected to beat us. But if you play 100 per cent, you have nothing to fear from these guys.'
Former Peru striker **Teofilo Cubillas**, 1994.

Scotland's 1990 World Cup campaign was a disaster with a difference. Frustrated by past embarrassments and determined that the squad would not be visited by the mismanagement and inflated hype of past campaigns, the SFA, with the meticulous ex-school teacher Andy Roxburgh at the helm, travelled to Italy with dignity and decorum. Unfortunately, the team went with them.
Stuart Cosgrove, *Hampden Babylon: Sex and Scandal in Scottish Football*, 1991.

At the moment the final whistle is blown on our hopes I fucking hate Emlyn Hughes, Nick Owen, Uruguay, England, Ireland, Hans Van Breukelen for messing up an easy save against Ireland, Jimmy Hill, Colombia and especially that bastard Valderrama, the Germans for not trying against Colombia, the bastard Austrian who refereed our match with Brazil, the Brazilian team for being completely hopeless and still beating us, Neil Simpson, Elton Welsby, Elton John, Ben Elton, Ben Nevis, Big Ben, Big Tel, Gary Lineker's toe, Gary Gilmore's eyes, football, the World Cup, the thought of having to go through all this again in four years' time, everybody, myself.
Alastair McSporran venting spleen as Scotland go out of Italia '90, *The Absolute Game* fanzine, September 1990.

EUROPE

We fancied our chances of getting to Hampden, but that thought lasted about five minutes into the first leg against Eintracht. They were so quick, and they killed us at our own game, which was wingers. At half-time it was one each, and they had missed a penalty, but in the second half we didn't know whether we were coming or going . . . I didn't really feel I had been in a game because I only touched the ball about 20 times in the match. We lost 6–1 but honestly it could have been 10.

Rangers wing-half **Willie Stevenson** on facing Eintracht Frankfurt in the 1960 European Cup semi-final. (Rangers lost the return 6–3 and Stevenson, refusing to believe a team who'd scored 12 against Rangers could lose, put £5 on them to beat Real Madrid.)

For his services at Hampden on the occasion of the first European Cup final ever staged in Scotland, Mowat was paid one shilling and sixpence – 7½p – to meet the cost of a rail fare to Hampden from the station nearest his home.

Russell Galbraith, *The Hampden Story*, 1993. Jack Mowat refereed the 1960 European Cup final between Real Madrid and Eintracht Frankfurt.

I don't think any of us wanted the referee to end the match, and I think that was true of the crowd also.

Real winger **Francisco Gento** on the 1960 European Cup final, *The European Cup, 1955–1980*.

I lined up for the first game and there was two men on Joe [Baker] and two on me. Our team played the same way. It was rubbish, it really was.

Dennis Law on playing for Torino, *Only a Game?*, BBC documentary, 1985.

Scotland were playing Uruguay at Hampden and we were playing Napoli in the quarter-finals of the Italian Cup, and if we won we had to play in Rome the same time as the Scotland game. I said I wanted to play for Scotland against Uruguay. He [the coach] said 'Well, if we win, you can't go.' Well . . . I won't say I didn't try. A professional could never say that. But

halfway through the game I got taken off and banned from the club for a fortnight.
Denis Law's Italian memories, *Only a Game?*, BBC documentary, 1985.

He [Stein] certainly underrated them [Feyenoord] and every player I have talked to from that team would admit it.
Archie MacPherson on Celtic's 1970 European Cup final defeat, *Action Replays*, 1991.

We knew what would await us in Spain. Wave upon wave of hatred whipped up by a vicious press campaign founded on absolute dishonesty and hypocrisy.
Jock Stein on the second leg of the European Cup tie against Atletico Madrid, April 1974. Atletico had three players sent off in the first leg at Parkhead.

Alex Ferguson pulled me into the squad for the away leg in Bulgaria and even gave me £5 a day spending money for the three-day trip. But whoever I was due to replace declared himself fit at the last minute and I was left behind. To add insult to injury, Fergie demanded the £15 back!
Aberdeen defender **Alex McLeish** on his 1978 European debut against Marek Stanke Dimitrov, October 1993.

I know enough now to know Scotland are not going to put six goals past us.
Luxembourg boss **Paul Phillip** after watching Eire play Scotland in Dublin, October 1986.

There used to be gentlemen in British football, but there are none at Ibrox.
Dynamo Kiev spokesman after Rangers reduced the width of the Ibrox pitch against them for a European Cup tie, October 1987.

People really have the wrong idea about how the game is played in Germany. They reckon it's 100 mph stuff, performed by muscular athletes who can run all day. Nothing could be further from the truth. The Germans don't play strict man-for-man marking. There's almost an unwritten law which says, 'You let our play-maker play and we'll do the same for you.'
Murdo MacLeod on his Bundesliga experiences with Borussia Dortmund, 1992.

If anyone turns up late for training [in Italy] it's really frowned upon; you have let yourself and your team-mates down. Once I got caught in a traffic jam at New Year, when I'd been with my family, and I was fined £5000 for being two hours late.
Graeme Souness, 1991.

Romania became rapidly disheartened at being shown up by a lesser side, suffered the loss of an equaliser and then the ultimate absurdity of a Motherwell player dispossessing one of Europe's finest, Hagi of Real Madrid, to help set up a Scotland winner.
Rab Crangle on the Scotland v Romania European Championship qualifier, The Absolute Game fanzine, March 1992.

A backs-to-the-wall draw in Sofia was followed by a return match with Bulgaria which was more typical of the type of match Scots fans had been used to since the mid-1980s. Shite.
Rab Crangle on the 1992 European Championship campaign, The Absolute Game fanzine, March 1992.

I learned more in my first three months with Ajax than in five years with Spurs. Coaching there is a science. You'd train for 10 minutes, then Cruyff would stop and discuss it for 20.
Ajax's Scottish winger **Ally Dick**, June 1992.

The noise level when we came on to the pitch was as loud as I've ever heard. But within a minute it was as quiet as I've ever known.
Ally McCoist recalling the early Leeds goal against them in the European Cup tie at Ibrox, 1992.

I saw the corner come over and realised Dave McPherson had every chance of getting in a header on goal. So before the ball even reached Dave, I ran straight at the keeper, jinked to avoid my marker, and when the header was blocked by Lukic I was there to knock the rebound home. I took a chance, played a hunch if you like, and it came off. The next day, most of the papers described it along the lines of, '. . . and McCoist had a simple job to score from close range . . .' Possibly true, but I like to think the hard work was done getting me into the position that made the act of scoring look simple.
Ally McCoist, recalling his goal for Rangers v Leeds at Ibrox, 1992.

The noise when we came on to the pitch at Ibrox in the first leg was incredible, but there was silence after a minute's play. Leeds got a corner and I was supposed to be standing on the 18-yard box, where Gary McAllister hit a volley into the net. As he ran past, he patted me on the backside and said, 'What about that for a wee strike?' At Elland Road I scored with a header and as I passed him I did the same and said, 'What about that for a wee header?' He who laughs last laughs loudest.

Ally McCoist on the European Cup ties with Leeds, 1992.

We call it the BFG. It was a boot down the middle, a flick on and a goal.

Mark Hateley, recalling his goal against Leeds in the European Cup at Elland Road, 1993.

It was like trying to carry a ton weight up the down escalator. Goram, outstanding. Gough, outstanding. Brown, in many ways, outstanding. You wonder how Scotland could ever lose a football match.

Leeds boss **Howard Wilkinson** after Rangers had knocked them out of the European Cup, 1992.

The Russians [CSKA Moscow] were claiming that they had been drugged, that their food in the hotel had been tampered with. The accusations, at that time, were not being made in public. But in France they were known to everyone in football . . . We were staying in one of the best hotels in the South of France and yet we brought our own food, our own drinking water and our own chefs to make absolutely certain that no one could get near the food the players were eating . . . it's a fairly normal procedure for a club to take food to trips to Eastern Europe . . . but in a country which prides itself on its food and its cooking, it was stranger to see a team arrive with enough hampers to cater for every meal the lads took during their stay there . . . When I played for Monaco there were always rumours flying around, always gossip about the goings-on at the Marseille club, but in the main I put it down to jealousy over their high-profile president, Bernard Tapie.

Mark Hateley, *Top Mark!*, 1993.

We'll walk on to that park on Wednesday knowing we're the envy of every professional footballer in Britain.

Rangers defender **John Brown** before the Champions' League match against Marseille, April 1993.

It always gets back to the same question for me. Could a former electrician from Carmyle win the European Cup?

Walter Smith, 1993.

Being undefeated in ten European Cup ties and still not reaching the final would be a typically Scottish way to miss out.

Prescient Rangers striker **Ally McCoist** before the final Champions' League tie with CSKA Moscow, April 1993. That was what happened.

VISITING TEAM

The Scots were in seventh heaven but it was amusing to note grown men kissing each other. Hugging and handshaking and kissing at a football match – is it any wonder that foreigners deny we of our race can keep our emotions in hand?
Trevor Wignall, *Daily Express*, after a Tommy Walker penalty at Wembley had clinched the Home International Championship for Scotland, April 1936.

I played trials for Fiorentina then moved to Brescia, a Fourth Division club, where I stayed for a year. I'd to do my military service as a paratrooper and during that time I trained with Pisa and played for them in training against Fiorentina, Inter Milan and Napoli. But I began to feel homesick and came back to Scotland.
Largs-born Dumbarton keeper **Alessandro Fontana**, holder of one of Scottish football's more interesting CVs, September 1984.

Old habits die hard, so I've been trying to persuade them to change their red and white colours to blue.
Seville boss **Jock Wallace**, December 1986.

In principle, I feel all the tasks the manager set me I fulfilled to my own and his satisfaction.
Oleg Kuznetsov, Ukrainian international, after his debut for Rangers, October 1990.

The only problem he had was that his cigar smoke kept getting in his eyes.
Team-mate **Ally McCoist** on Kuznetsov in the same game.

That was one of the best marking jobs ever done on me. Gough was outstanding. He went to the limit against me without a booking.
Holland striker **Marco Van Basten** after facing Scotland in the European Championships, June 1992.

The major upset of the tournament was of course Pat Nevin being pipped in the Pat Nevin Lookalike Contest by Christian

Perez of France. In almost every respect they were evenly matched – gifted creative genuises; never played a full 90 minutes; decent haircuts; hardly a shot on target; permanent melancholy expression. In the end, though, what tipped the balance in Perez's favour was the fact he played for a team that returned home with shame and humiliation raining down on them. Can't win 'em all, Pat.

The Absolute Game fanzine on the European Championships, August 1992.

Alexei is, well, Alexei. He has great economy of movement.

Rangers boss and diplomat, **Walter Smith** on Alexei Mikhailitchenko, Rangers AGM, 1993.

He said it was something he envied about British football – the ability to come into a ground and just switch on the aggression.

Ex-Ajax Scot **Ally Dick** on Johann Cruyff, June 1992.

I was Yugoslavian. Suddenly, you hear all this about separate peoples from so-called intelligent beings. That is one reason why in my house we don't want to see the news. It is too painful.

Dundee United's Croatian boss, **Ivan Golac**, October 1993.

My job is to have sweepers thinking about me, but when we played Italy at Ibrox I was thinking about him [Franco Baresi]. It's the only time that has happened.

Ally McCoist, February 1994.

FANS

A newspaper published a letter from a viewer comparing our coverage to 'filming with a Brownie whilst jumping on a trampoline'.

Archie MacPherson, recalling the BBC's filming of the 1965 League Cup semi-final between Rangers and Kilmarnock, *Action Replays*, 1991.

We got into our dressing-room that day making plenty of noise, only to find that we had been beaten into the bath by two blokes wearing the lion rampant as dressing-gowns. The team were not at all unhappy with sharing the soap with a couple of the paying public, but the Metropolitan police were less than pleased and huffily carried off our bathing companions.

Danny McGrain recalling Scotland's 1981 Wembley win over England, *In Sunshine or in Shadow*, 1987.

Communism v Alcoholism.

Scottish fans' banner at Soviet Union v Scotland World Cup match, 1982.

I was never popular with the Scottish crowd. I played once for Scotland against Wales and got booed every time I touched the ball. I was upset because I was proud to play for Scotland but the crowd's reaction only acted as a spur.

Graeme Souness,1989.

I can't really blame Carole. She never understood my passion for Celtic and we had a lot of rows because I was always away. Following the lads takes nearly all my money and my mates say I'm crazy. But I don't care. I just can't give it up.

Glenn Bonnell, Celts fan from Penwortham, Lancs (190 miles from Glasgow). His wife gave him an ultimatum in 1984, after 11 years as a football widow. (Quoted in *Great Sporting Eccentrics* by David Randall.)

If Cammy scores a hat-trick he can make that gesture to me. He just celebrates that way and I feel the fans may have misinterpreted his excitement.

Rangers manager **Jock Wallace** after Cammy Fraser made a V sign at Rangers fans who'd been barracking him against St Mirren, 15 December 1984.

The worst sort of Hibs supporter is the one who says he wants Hearts to win the league if Hibs can't win it. He is lying in his teeth. He is a hypocrite.
John Fairgrieve, *The Boys in Maroon*, 1986.

The Scottish public come to an international with a great sense of pride and when they are chanting 'What a load of rubbish' it just might be that I'm chanting along with them down on the bench.
Andy Roxburgh, November 1986.

Who the fuck's Andy Walker?
Celtic fans' response to Motherwell supporters' calls for the player to be introduced as a sub, Skol Cup semi-final, 23 September 1986. Walker came on and scored as Motherwell fought back to draw 2–2. He eventually joined Celtic.

In Glasgow half the fans hate you and the other half think they own you.
Celtic's **Tommy Burns**, 1987.

I don't know what he said because I don't speak the same language.
Celtic's **Brian McClair** on the Rangers fan who ran up to him during an Old Firm game, April 1987.

Jock Stein used to sum up the Old Firm supporters in this way: when Rangers had a good result and you congratulated one of their followers, he would say, 'What's it got to do with you?' When you said the same thing to a Celtic man, he asked you what you wanted to drink.
Danny McGrain, *In Sunshine or in Shadow*, 1987.

In the first round, Rangers were drawn against Dynamo Kiev but the Soviet authorities wouldn't grant visas to travelling fans. This, of course, was no barrier to a group of resourceful Teddy Bears, who joined the Scottish Communist Party, successfully applied for a tour of Kiev and mentioned that they would quite like to take in a football match, should such an event be taking place.
Roddy Forsyth, *Glasgow Rangers Revisited: a 120-Year History*.

The day will come when I will have to miss a European tie, but I would rather it was at a time of my own choosing.
Rangers fan **Robert McElroy**, announcing his intention to travel to Kiev to watch Rangers in the European Cup despite having been refused a visa, September 1987.

I can remember taking my seat at Hampden before a Scotland match and being picked out by a spectator who was obviously not a Celtic supporter. 'McGrain, ya Fenian bastard!' he shouted up at me before he realised the description was inaccurate and changed his insult to, 'McGrain, ya diabetic bastard!'
Danny McGrain, *Celtic Greats*, 1988.

'Ally, Ally, get to ****, Ally, get to ****.' It was 16 February 1985, without a doubt the worst day of my football life . . . Rangers were on their way to a 1–0 Scottish Cup defeat by Dundee. I was having a real stinker of a game and the Rangers fans were letting me know in no uncertain terms what they thought of my efforts.
Ally McCoist in *My Story*, 1992.

I heard this bloke in the stand shouting, 'McGraw [Allan manager], we're fucking sick of what you're doing to Morton, buying bastards like Gahagan.' Two minutes later I scored what turned out to be the winner and as I was running back I heard the same guy shouting, 'Yes, Johnny boy, gie's another one!'
Morton's **John Gahagan**, 1990.

Crowds don't come to be bored. I don't set out to be deliberately eye-catching, but if I can entertain them by doing things spontaneously, who's complaining?
Falkirk's **Simon Stainrod**, April 1991.

In 1991 I was home and stripping wallpaper well before six o'clock.
Dundee United official historian and Glasgow Central MP **Mike Watson**, on his method of dealing with United's Cup final misfortunes. 1991 was their sixth losing final.

In 1991 we all went to the final wearing these cardboard headdresses in honour of United's nickname, the Arabs. As we

watched the team losing, it rained and all the colours started to run down our faces . . . They'll probably win when I'm not there and I'll have to name the baby after the entire team.
GMTV presenter and pregnant Dundee United fan **Lorraine Kelly**, February 1994.

He's white, he's blue, he shat in Simon's shoe.
Falkirk fans chant at Dens Park, August 1992. Falkirk signing Ian McCall had been freed by Dundee during a pre-season tour after an unsavoury prank involving manager Simon Stainrod's boots.

I did something which was wrong but a lot of footballers do things which are wrong . . . But I must say it has not altered my admiration for Simon Stainrod.
Ian McCall on the incident, March 1993.

We're blue, we're white, we're absolutely shite, Queen of the South.
Chant by Palmerston fans, 1990–91 season.

One thinks of the mass paranoia exhibited by thousands of Rangers supporters singing in unison, 'Everybody hates us and we don't care.' This, of course, is not true paranoia in the medical sense, since the essence of the illness is that the fear of persecution is unfounded in fact, while as we all know, in reality everybody does hate Rangers.
Alastair McSporran, *The Absolute Game* fanzine, April 1991.

The fans gave us pelters and pelters is what we deserved.
Celtic boss **Liam Brady** after a 0–0 draw with Kilmarnock, October 1993.

I want to be banned from watching Celtic.
Celtic fan **Martin McCallum**, explaining to police why he'd attacked Rangers goalkeeper Ally Maxwell after 28 minutes of the Old Firm match, 1 January 1994. Celtic were 3–0 down at the time. He subsequently got his wish and was also jailed for two months.

It was the worst game I've ever seen as a Celtic supporter. I just couldn't believe what I was watching.
Partick Thistle midfielder (and Celtic fan) **Chic Charnley** on the Ne'erday Old Firm defeat by Rangers, January 1994.

PLAYERS

I'm not sharp enough to be a top-class striker and my record bears me out. I've always managed to score in the lower divisions, but once I step up – kaput!
Kilmarnock striker **John Bourke**, August 1979. He'd scored 23 goals in 30 games the previous season.

I played with Denis [Law] with Scotland, then the following week I played against him for Manchester United. I thought, 'I'm playing against Denis, if I go for a 50–50 ball, I'll take it easy, he's my big pal.' Christ, he nearly killed me. I said, 'Den, what are you doing?' All he said was, 'No friends on the park, son.' And that was a lesson I remembered through my life.
Billy Bremner, Only a Game?, BBC documentary, 1985.

Bobby Murdoch in midfield gives them an aura of calm, presenting an illusion that they are impregnable. That is his great ability, to be composed on the ball. He isn't fast, he isn't strong in the tackle, he doesn't hit a great long ball, he can't beat a man. But what he is great at – when everyone else in this Division is going at ninety miles an hour, hitting imposs-ible balls, trying to squeeze things into spaces when it just is not on – is being composed, and slowing it down. Knocking the 15- or 20-yard ball, getting it back, and knocking it again. For half an hour I ran myself ragged jockeying Murdoch, who would push it to Souness or Foggon. They would knock it forward at the moment I lunged, committed to yet another fruitless tackle.
Eamon Dunphy on Murdoch playing for Middlesbrough, Only a Game?, 1976.

Martin Buchan, who was a complex character at the best of times and hardly a calming influence when there was unrest off the field, came storming out of his room and stalked into the foyer telling anyone who was interested that he was going straight back home again because his hotel room was too small. Ally's way of calming troubled waters was to tell Martin that he could take his room instead, rather than telling him that if

this was how he felt on the eve of representing his country in the World Cup a return ticket could easily be arranged . . . Discipline deteriorated very quickly after that.
Danny McGrain on Argentina '78, *In Sunshine or in Shadow*, 1987.

We have a working relationship. They do what they like and I take the credit when we win and blame them when we get beat.
Dundee United boss **Jim McLean** on players, *Only a Game?*, BBC documentary, 1985.

I've got high hopes for Gary McAllister. He has the best potential and technique I've seen in a young player for ages, and has the ability to become the next Graeme Souness.
Motherwell manager **Tommy McLean** on McAllister, then a teenager playing in the First Division, May 1985.

I'd to convert Andy Walker from a winger to a centre-forward. He didn't fancy it at first and was never out of my office asking to go back to the wing.
Tommy McLean, May 1985.

The most complete player in British football, the best two-footed player in the game, [but] not exactly a deep thinker.
Mark Lawrenson on Steve Nicol, 1988.

'Chipsy' [Steve Nicol] jumped on the machine only to see the needle swing way past his required weight to more than a stone in excess. He demanded to know if the scales were wrong, failing to understand the shop assistant's choked and negative reply, until his long-suffering wife pointed out that he was still carrying the shopping.
Graeme Souness, *No Half Measures*, 1985.

Playing me at centre-forward always raises a few eyebrows. It might surprise people to know it's my favourite position. I've played there eight or nine times and have always felt comfortable.
Pat Nevin, October 1986.

If Davie Cooper was playing on the continent he'd be a millionaire and retired by now.
Graeme Souness, October 1986.

He doesn't have the hunger that typifies people like Andy Gray and Richard Gough, and that used to infuriate me. But I've given up now. You can't change his nature. And at the top level there's no way you can survive without players of his natural ability.
Jim McLean on David Narey, December 1986.

Better than Gary Lineker and more dangerous than Maurice Johnston.
Terry Butcher on Brian McClair, February 1987.

Scottish players don't seem to be interested in improving their technique. They want as much as they can get for as little as possible. I have one player here who got into a crossing position six times last night – four of them were bad crosses. Yet not once has this individual volunteered to come back to the ground to work on this fault. I'm going downstairs into the dressing-room to ask why this is so. Players will work on the things they are good at but they are loath to sort out their faults. I'll assure you that the individual will be back to work on his flaws. Unfortunately, I doubt if he will volunteer. He will have to be given an order.
Jim McLean after Dundee United had lost 4–0 at home to Vitesse Arnhem in the UEFA Cup, 8 October 1990.

At half-time I was suggesting to Henrik he might like to put in a bit more effort. He pointed at the sky and said, 'Too hot to run.' Henrik was on his way back to Denmark within 24 hours.
Dundee boss **Jim Duffy** on striker Henrik Nielsen, freed the day Duffy took over, September 1993.

At Tannadice, he didn't have any kind of reputation for talking back, but since coming here he's never shut up. I've tried everything – fining him, telling him straight he was letting people down, whipping him off after being booked. But nothing seems to work. The problem seems to be that Darren gets so caught up in games that half the time he doesn't know what he's doing and saying. I've had him in my office on a Monday and he's stood and argued that he never did the things I was fining him for. He's been so adamant that I've had to threaten to show him the video of the match before he'll accept what he's done.

Hibs boss **Alex Miller** on striker Darren Jackson (16 bookings and a red card in 15 months at Easter Road), October 1993.

Being freed isn't a condemnation, it's only another manager's opinion. I was at Motherwell when Brian McClair came to us on a free from Aston Villa. Peter Beardsley, David Platt, Eoin Jess – they were all once in the same boat.

Scotland boss **Craig Brown**, preparing to pick Motherwell defender **Rob McKinnon**, who was once freed by Newcastle, November 1993.

In Scotland, the toughest defenders I've played against have been Willie Miller and Alex McLeish. I've broken my nose against both of them.

Ally McCoist, February 1994.

Billy Bremner is Scottish football in miniature. If FIFA ever gets round to creating an identikit picture of national footballing types, the Scottish player will be short, stocky, aggressive and ginger-haired. He will have a fiery temper, a bad disciplinary record and a passionate spirit. He will come from a rough housing scheme in Stirling and his name will be Billy Bremner.

Stuart Cosgrove, *Hampden Babylon: Sex and Scandal in Scottish Football*, 1991.

He'd have a mixture of Billy Bremner arrogance – small and hard – Kenny Dalglish brilliance, Denis Law, the best-ever goalscorer, Dave Mackay, diehard, desperate will-to-win . . . and he'd also have a floppy pair of hands.

Emlyn Hughes on the identikit Scottish footballer, *Only a Game?*, BBC documentary, 1985.

He isn't going to set the world on fire and he's maybe not the type who'll have fans drooling.

Celtic boss **Lou Macari** on new signing, Willie Falconer of Sheffield United, February 1994.

Walter Smith told me if he could guarantee ten other players who shared Mark's enthusiasm, passion and hunger, he would have the league won from the first day of the season.
Tony Hateley, father of Mark, March 1994.

GOALKEEPERS

Goalkeeper Chic McIntosh was to become a personality. Although only 5' 7" tall, his lack of height was more than offset by great agility and safe handling . . . Whenever possible he would dive full-length to hold the ball. Even though on many occasions a simple pick-up was all that was needed. Equally, when the ball was at the opposite end he thought nothing of having a chat through the net with spectators, relying on them to let him know if play began to shift downfield.
Mike Watson, *Rags to Riches: the Official History of Dundee United*, 1985.

My first final was 11 years ago and I wasn't in the least nervous. In fact, I spent the day before learning to canoe on Loch Lomond. You probably get more perturbed as you get older.
Aberdeen's **Bobby Clark** before the 1978 Scottish Cup final.

What's the point in breaking off in mid-season to do pre-season training?
Morton's American international keeper **Dave Brcic**, January 1979. New York Cosmos wanted him to go to Trinidad to stay fit, but he confirmed the goalkeepers/crazy theory by opting to winter in Greenock.

I'm roughly the same height and build as Muhammad Ali and you wouldn't call him less than an athlete, would you?
Bobby McKell, 6' 4", 15 st 7 lb Falkirk keeper, February 1979. At the time Liverpool's Ray Clemence was the only goalkeeper in Britain with a better record.

I'm even more dedicated in training now than I was in London. Living on Mull you have to be.
Dundee United keeper **Peter Bonetti**, September 1979. He had a short (five games) spell at Tannadice after 20 years with Chelsea.

I developed a liking for pickled onions and would eat entire jars. I liked them so much I started to drink the vinegar left in

the bottle. On one occasion it made me so ill I'd to be rushed to hospital to have my stomach pumped.
Celtic reserve keeper **Alan Davidson**, May 1980.

We lost my first game 6–3 and I remember saying to my mother when I got home that I wouldn't be asked to play for them again.
Queen of the South keeper **Allan Ball**, September 1981, on his early days with the club. He made over 800 appearances for them in 18 years.

Up at Tannadice,
Framed in woodwork, cool as ice
Keeping out the wolves in his particular way
A smile and a wave, a miraculous save they say
Out runs Hamish and the ball's in Invergowrie Bay.
Michael Marra's song, *Hamish*, 1991.

The people who have criticised me for failing to stop John Robertson's free-kick last Saturday don't know the first thing about goalkeeping. I'd like to take them out on to a park and ask them to show me where I was standing when the kick was taken. I'd guarantee not one of them could tell me where I was actually positioned.
Celtic's **Pat Bonner**, February 1987.

Goalkeepers in Scotland are notorious as 'goal-liners'. If you want them to come off their line you almost have to prise them out with a crowbar. We have asked Packie to be a sweeper.
Eire boss **Jack Charlton**, 1991.

Hello, this is Scotland's top goalkeeper.
Message on **John Burridge**'s answering-machine, 1991.

I've seen him eating jars of baby food before games because he believes it increases his carbohydrate level. But he works harder than anyone I've ever seen in football – and has more belief in himself than anyone I've ever met in football. He used to describe himself with the words, 'I'm as fit as a butcher's dog' – and he is.
Reading boss **Mark McGhee** on Burridge, his former Newcastle team-mate, 1991.

Had he not gone for a career in football, I don't think there is any doubt that he would have gone on to make the grade as a county cricketer.

South of Scotland Cricket Association secretary Gordon Fraser, after **Andy Goram** joined Kelso Cricket Club, 1991.

When I went to Oldham at first, Andy was a hooligan. He wasn't living right off the park and his attitude wasn't too great.

Goalkeeping coach **Alan Hodgkinson** on Andy Goram, November 1992.

People always bring up the fact that he's only 5' 11" – supposedly small for a keeper. I played in the English First Division for 20 years and I'm smaller than Andy. It's a fallacy that keepers have to be big, a complete myth.

Alan Hodgkinson on Andy Goram, November 1992.

I have been in the Republic's team since 1981 and I've never felt as exposed as I did on Wednesday. There is a tension among a small element of the crowd that a Celtic player gets used to during a game at Ibrox, for instance, but Windsor Park was hardline extremism.

Celtic keeper **Pat Bonner** after Eire's draw in Belfast ensured World Cup qualification, 18 November 1993.

SUPERALLY

NAME: Alistair McCoist. Class: 4K.
Dear Parent, your son/daughter was late on Thursday morning/afternoon for no apparent reason. In such situations the school imposes a standard punishment to be completed on this sheet and signed by yourself. Rewrite the following statement 25 times: 'Punctuality is the first step in the learning process of the schoolday.'

Extract from punishment exercise given to fourth-year pupil **McCoist** at Hunter High School, East Kilbride, 1978. (Many throughout the land would question whether the punishment took effect.)

When you see it on video it's quite funny. There's wee Ally McCoist in the corner of the screen hooking one of their players and then running away. The players concerned turns round, sees Colin West, and takes a swing at him. And so it went on.

Ex-Ranger **Stuart Munro**, January 1994, on Graeme Souness's Rangers debut against Hibs, August 1986. Both clubs were later fined for their parts in the centre-circle brawl.

I'd taken a couple of hefty whacks from Mark Fulton during the game and when the flare-up began in the centre-circle I decided that was my opportunity to get a bit of revenge with a sly little dink at him. Of course the TV cameras caught me in the act and showed it for what it was – cheap and nasty . . . I'm really ashamed of the incident. It was sneaky and devious. I cringe at the memory.

Ally McCoist on the same match, *My Story.*

I scored a goal in a Cup tie at Ayr a couple of weeks ago. Once again, a tap-in from close range after the keeper had blocked a shot. This punter came up to me in a pub afterwards and said: 'You got your money easy today, they can't come any simpler than that.' I could have got annoyed, but I just laughed. He hadn't a clue about what had gone on in the five seconds before that put me in the position for the tap-in.

Ally McCoist, February 1993.

I'm not looking for accolades but I think some people take my goalscoring for granted . . . I think it's that old Scottish characteristic of building someone up so you can shoot them down. You know what I mean – Allan Wells only won gold in Moscow because the Americans weren't there; the field was weaker than normal the year Sandy Lyle won the Open. I'm not the first it has happened to and I won't be the last.
Ally McCoist, February 1993.

I have absolutely no doubt that he [Souness] would have sold me in season 1990–91 when the Hateley-Johnston partnership was going so well.
Ally McCoist, *My Story.*

I never had any intention of selling McCoist and I never would have. There was never any animosity between us. People have tried to make out I did not like him and that I was jealous of him. That was all rubbish.
Graeme Souness, September 1992.

'You were a dud at St Johnstone,' he [Souness] shouted. 'You were a dud at Sunderland, and you're still a f***ing dud.' Ian Durrant promptly christened me 'Dudley'.
Ally McCoist, *My Story.*

In those days when the stick was flying, there were three players who, to my mind, seemed to get more than their fair share – Stuart Munro, Ian Durrant, and Ally McCoist. Of course, we had something in common – we hadn't been signed by Souness.
Ally McCoist, *My Story.*

There are players on our staff – I think mostly ones I inherited – who are afraid when they get out on to Ibrox because of the size of the crowd.
Graeme Souness after the Scottish Cup defeat by Hamilton, 31 January 1987.

The gaffer said to me after the Cup final: 'You're a lucky bastard. I don't mean for scoring that goal. I just mean you're a lucky bastard generally.'

Ally McCoist after his first goal following a broken leg won the League Cup for Rangers with an acrobatic overhead kick, November 1993.

You can be lucky once or twice, but I don't think you can be lucky 49 times. It's gambling, it's instinct, it's timing. A goal's like a good joke, it's like delivering a punchline at exactly the right moment.
Ally McCoist, November 1993.

I am officially the worst header of a ball in Britain.
Ally McCoist, November 1993.

The last three years have been unbelievable for me. I wake up every morning and I think I'm the luckiest man alive. I'm coming in here. It's not work, is it? I'd be doing it anywhere, just training and playing with my mates for fun. I love it. I really love it.
Ally McCoist, November 1993.

He [McCoist] would be in my all-time list of greats. He would be with Virdis and Rossi and Lineker and all the others and let's not have any criticism about him scoring goals in a lesser league. I won't have that. Our league in Scotland is as competitive as you can get anywhere. Besides, scoring goals is difficult in any league and at any level . . . The goals against Leeds . . . must have shut up a few big-mouths who like to take a pop at us with all the insults about the standards up in Scotland. My answer to them is: come and try it. Then they would know the demands placed on players with Rangers. They are as high as you will get anywhere in the world.
Mark Hateley, *Top Mark!*, 1993.

Ally definitely gets taken a bit for granted. To some extent Rangers as a club suffer from it, but it's particularly noticeable with him. He will break every scoring record at this club. I'm convinced of that. But lately there's been a feeling that his misses rather than his goals get highlighted . . . Rangers fans should think back eight years and ask themselves if they preferred a team which wasn't successful – but a team in which Ally McCoist was still top scorer.
Rangers boss **Walter Smith**, March 1993. At the time, McCoist had scored 282 goals in 438 games for Rangers.

I was thrilled until I learned Ivan Lendl had finished above me.
Ally McCoist on being named fifth best-looking sportsman in the world, 1990.

He's handsome, he's rich, he's funny and he's happy – my envy knows no bounds.
Billy Connolly, in the foreword to *Ally McCoist: My Story*, 1991.

Maybe ten or twenty years from now people will look back and say, 'That McCoist scored some number of goals.'
Ally McCoist, March 1993.

ANGLOS

He [Denis Law] had stopped trying. A typical example of the way I found things with him at United was this: he would be injured on the Saturday after the game. He would sometimes come in for treatment on the Sunday, sometimes not. He'd be in for treatment Monday, Tuesday, Wednesday and Thursday, a loosener up on the Friday, and be ready for Saturday. I smelled it a mile away.
Tommy Docherty on arriving at Old Trafford in 1972, *Call the Doc*, 1981.

I dislike Pat Crerand. His envy of greater talents (like Bobby Charlton's) was always clear to me.
Tommy Docherty, *Call the Doc*, 1981.

As an enemy, Doc was vicious, vindictive and callous.
Pat Crerand, on Tommy Docherty.

10 st of Barbed Wire.
Sunday Times headline on profile of **Billy Bremner**, 1970.

Above all, [Leeds] have Bremner, the best footballer in the four countries. If every manager in Britain were given his choice of any one player to add to his team some, no doubt, would toy with the idea of Best; but the realists, to a man, would have Bremner.
John Arlott, journalist, *The Guardian*, 1970.

Bruce [Rioch] had a military bearing about him as well as an English accent that would have made him unintelligible to the vast majority of Scotland supporters, but I have never met a man who took such pride in playing for his country or who thought so deeply about the game. He was often my room-mate on international trips and a more civilised person you could not wish to meet.
Danny McGrain, *In Sunshine or in Shadow*, 1987.

An odd young man.
Graeme Souness on Steve Archibald, *No Half Measures*, 1985.

In one match I watched he hardly broke out of a walk for 90 minutes. I was longing for someone to have a run at him, but no one ever did. He was such a good reader of the play, he was outstanding at that level.

Liverpool chief scout Geoff Twentyman on Alan Hansen, February 1983.

Jim McInally, the former Forest full-back, was particularly unremitting in his criticism of Clough's methods and earned a few bob from *The Sun* for his disclosures. Shortly after McInally's transfer to Coventry, Clough spotted a log floating down the Trent during a training session and lined his team up on the riverbank to salute it. As the flotsam glided past, Clough announced to his bemused troops, 'There goes Jim McInally – let that be a warning to you!'

Tony Francis, *Clough – A Biography*, 1987.

For three or four years I couldn't wait for Saturday. Just to get out there was a joy. I wanted to play for him. Sounds soppy but it's true.

John Robertson on the Clough years at Forest. (Quoted in *Clough – A Biography* by Tony Francis, 1987.)

He was a very unattractive young man. If ever I felt off colour I'd sit next to him, because compared to this fat, dumpy lad I was Errol Flynn. But give him a ball and a yard of grass and he was an artist. He was the Picasso of our game.

Brian Clough on John Robertson, in the *Cloughie* video, 1990.

He wanted me to take responsibility for the ball, to do something worthwhile with it. Moral courage, he called it – he said ten-yard passes were fiddling, farty things.

John Robertson on Clough.

I have never known anyone eat so much before a game. Most players are careful with their diet. I will probably sip a Perrier or eat a bag of crisps a couple of hours before kick-off, but not Nico. He eats anything he can get his hands on. Sweets, biscuits, nuts, crisps, chocolates, pints of milk, coke, anything. On the Saturday before we played Everton he had a meal at Anfield before we left for the hotel, which is only about 50 minutes away. But no sooner had we entered our room than Nico contacted room service to order a club sandwich. Dinner was at 6.30 but that didn't stop the club sandwiches coming up from the kitchen at regular intervals. He eventually fell asleep while I was watching *Match of the Day*, then suddenly awoke, sat up in bed and shouted, 'Any crisps? Any crisps?' then just went back to sleep. The man's mad ... At five o'clock I was suddenly awoken by the bed rocking to and fro, and to my disbelief Nico was on his feet trying to push me out of bed. I had one foot on the floor and was screaming at him to pack it in and go back to bed. He was clearly still asleep and didn't have a clue what was going on. He thought I was joking when I told him in the morning.

John Aldridge on Steve Nicol, *Inside Anfield*, 1988.

Steve Nicol, a young player not long arrived from Ayr, was told by Graeme Souness and Alan Hansen that Dalglish was seriously ill. The team were on a tour of Israel and Dalglish had returned to bed for his usual afternoon nap.

'Have you noticed he doesn't train every day?' they pointed out, 'And goes home to sleep in an afternoon?' Nicol nodded.

'That's because he's got leukaemia,' added Souness, 'and what's more it's terminal.'

Nicol raced off to Dalglish's room, checking first with a few other Liverpool players who, of course, had been primed. In the meantime Ronnie Whelan rang Dalglish's room to put him in on the joke. Nicol knocked gently on Dalglish's door.

'Come in,' answered a quiet voice. Dalglish was lying in bed, doing his best to look ill.

'I've just heard about your illness,' said Nicol, almost in tears. 'I'm really sorry. I didn't know.'

'Aye, I'm afraid it's true,' confessed Dalglish. 'Hadn't you noticed how badly I've been playing recently?'

'Well, yes, I had actually,' began Nicol . . .

Stephen F. Kelly, *Dalglish*.

Nicol was frequently the butt of Dalglish and Souness's humour. Nicol, Dalglish and Souness were travelling up to Scotland in Souness's car for an international. The weather was atrocious: snow, sleet and bitterly cold, but Nicol, as was his wont, came dressed in only a tee-shirt . . . Souness stopped the car and asked Nicol to go out and wipe the back window as it was getting snowed up. Nicol happily piled out of the back and got on with it. But no sooner had he started scraping

the window than Souness slammed his foot down and tore away, leaving the young Scot stranded by the roadside yelling after them. Half an hour later they returned. Nicol was almost frozen solid.
Stephen F. Kelly, **Dalglish**.

I was blessed in those days, but Arsenal took it away from me.
Charlie Nicholas, 1990.

Arsenal had a certain style – not for nothing were they known as a boring side. They were defensive in attitude and, given the way I play, it was always going to be difficult to adapt.
Charlie Nicholas, October 1993.

People who didn't watch Arsenal regularly will say I wasn't a big hit, but I think if you were to ask the punters at Highbury they would tell you another story. They always liked me, and I must have done something to appeal to them. You don't get the sort of appreciation they showed me because you look good or dress well.
Charlie Nicholas, October 1993.

Leicester got the steal of a lifetime when they got him for £150,000.
Motherwell boss **Tommy McLean** on Gary McAllister, October 1993.

United have got the bargain of all time.
Celtic manager **Billy McNeill** after a tribunal fixed Brian McClair's fee to Manchester United at £850,000 – less than half Celtic's £2 million valuation, July 1987.

I don't know whether to laugh or cry. It's a lot of money, the most I've ever paid for a player.
Alex Ferguson, who'd offered £400,000 for McClair, 30 July 1987.

My favourite footballer ever.
Jimmy Greaves on Denis Law, quoted in *The Times*, November 1993.

Law at 15 was like a little whippet. And when he got the hare he shook it as well. He had eyes in the back of his head like

Finney had. Guts and ability, and determination. He had the lot.
Bill Shankly on Denis Law, *Only a Game?*, BBC documentary, 1985.

I never liked watching myself playing on television. I found it embarrassing. The character who was supposed to be me on the screen was not really me at all. He couldn't be, throwing a punch at someone, glaring at the linesman, arguing with the referee, and making rude signs. I didn't behave like that in real life. I could understand people watching me and saying 'What's he up to?'
Denis Law, November 1993

Denis Law, the Lawman, so-called because his second name was Law and he was a man. It was he who had the reactions of a mongoose, and the hairstyle as well.
It's Only an Excuse, BBC Radio Scotland spoof documentary, 1986.

Spurs.
Alfie Conn's answer when asked who he preferred playing for, Rangers or Celtic. He played for all three. *Only a Game*, BBC documentary, 1985.

At one game recently a guy was coming out with the usual lines, such as 'Where's your pension book and zimmer frame?' I just replied, 'Can't you do any better than that? I was getting those ones 15 years ago.'
Merthyr Tydfil winger **Tommy Hutchison**, still playing at 46, November 1993.

He has got himself into the most God Almighty muddle. He is not a worldly person. He is not financially astute.
Robert Fleck's solicitor, 1990. Fleck, brought to court on a charge of failing to make maintenance payments to his estranged wife, was revealed to be receiving £29 a week from Norwich, the remainder of his salary going to pay off debts.

Where's the crisis? If this is a crisis you should have been at some of the clubs I've been at.
David Speedie, Liverpool striker, after Kenny Dalglish's resignation, 1991.

I'm not in the picture so I didn't expect to be in the photo.
Newcastle midfielder **Roy Aitken** after being told to stay away from the club's pre-season photo-call, 1991.

I had to get rid of this idea that Manchester United were a drinking club rather than a football club.
Alex Ferguson on early problems at Old Trafford, *Six Years at United*, 1992.

This team makes you suffer. I deserve a million pounds a year to have this job.
Alex Ferguson after the drawn FA Cup final with Crystal Palace, 1990.

I can now understand why clubs come away from here having to bite their tongues and choking on their own vomit, knowing they have been done by referees. It would be a miracle to win here.
Alex Ferguson after Manchester United's draw at Anfield, where Colin Gibson was sent off, April 1988.

I signed four contracts at Liverpool and I was never any longer than five minutes making my mind up. That doesn't happen any more. And players don't reach as high a standard if they continually move as they would if they stayed at one club . . . Two or three new players a year take time to settle into a system, just as it takes time to settle into a new house.
Alan Hansen, April 1993.

When I was a teenager at Dundee and I saw the senior players I used to think, 'Well, if I'm with Arbroath at that age, getting £30 a week and all the kippers I can eat, I'll be doing pretty well for myself.'
Gordon Strachan, captaining Leeds at 33, 1990.

For a man so small in size he's a person of great stature who can destroy at once the big tough guys in the dressing-room with one lash of his coruscating tongue. That's why he earned the nickname 'King Tongue'.
Howard Wilkinson on Gordon Strachan, *Managing To Succeed: My Life in Football Management*, 1992.

I'm frightened to stop because there can be no life as enjoyable as this.
Gordon Strachan, 1992.

Sometimes, driving home from a game, you do wonder if you are getting old. But I always remember what Kenny Dalglish once told me: Never forget that football made you feel knackered when you were 17.
Gordon Strachan, 1992.

KENNY

My relationship with Kenny Dalglish did not get off to the best of starts mainly due to the fact that he thought I was a poof!
Graeme Souness, *No Half Measures*, 1985.

He [Dalglish] has been played off someone like Joe Jordan or Andy Gray [for Scotland], where at Liverpool they play off him. I tried it that way twice, when we played friendly games in Chile and Argentina before the 1978 World Cup finals. I used Kenny as a target man up front with little Lou Macari playing off him. It worked in both games and I'm only sorry I didn't persist. I thought of doing it against Iran, for instance, then changed my mind.
Ally MacLeod, quoted in *Dalglish* by Stephen F. Kelly.

Kenny, I would say, for three or four years was the best player in the world.
Graeme Souness, *Only a Game?*, BBC documentary, 1985.

Kenny calls all his goals 'tap-ins' until we come to the end of the season and we are talking money. Suddenly he changes his mind.
Bob Paisley, 1982.

The best player this club has signed this century.
Liverpool chairman **John Smith**, 1986.

I know he hates me. He's walked past me on the golf course as if I were a tree. He's the moaningest minnie I've ever known.
Birmingham boss **John Bond**, 1987.

Kenny's the best Liverpool player there's ever been, but playing against him never worried me. He never bothered me as a player. I could've marked him all day. I couldn't play against the likes of Martin Chivers. I couldn't see the ball, he was that big. But I could play against small, sharp, brainy players.
Emlyn Hughes, April 1987.

I never saw anyone in this country to touch him. I can think of only two who could go ahead of him. Pele, and possibly Cruyff.
Graeme Souness, 1988.

If Dalglish had been a Brazilian he would have played for Brazil, no question about it.
Bobby Robson

Kenny is intensely patriotic. While I pride myself on being British, he is purely and simply a Scot, fiercely proud of every Scottish achievement whether in sport or not.
Graeme Souness, *No Half Measures*, 1985.

He [Kenny] would have opinions – strong opinions, but he wouldn't offer them unless asked. But it was a different Kenny when the players were talking about conditions or whatever. In those meetings, he came on like a real Govan shipyard shop steward.
Graeme Souness, 1988.

People are a bit frightened of him. He growls at them. He makes them jump.
Graeme Souness after Dalglish got the Liverpool manager's job.

I went to watch Blackburn Rovers play Manchester United last season. I met him in the corridor and he stopped to talk to me. Believe it or not, I had butterflies.
Ally McCoist on Dalglish, February 1994.

Kevin [Keegan] was quicker off the mark, but Kenny runs the first five yards in his head.
Bob Paisley on Dalglish's sense of anticipation, 1981.

I used to think all that stuff about him running the first five yards in his head was rubbish until I'd played with him for a while.
Alan Hansen, 1992.

Pace isn't as important as people think. My wife could run faster than Kenny Dalglish.
Alan Hansen, April 1993.

Few great players make the transition into management. The reason is that great players are normally like soloists in an orchestra. They perform alone and tend to look down on team-mates with lesser ability. That was never Kenny Dalglish. He was like a conductor. He brought other players into play. He understood that not everyone was blessed with the greatest of skill. He had patience both as a player and a manager.
Bob Paisley, 1991.

Mind your own business.
Dalglish after being asked by a reporter if he'd criticised his players after a defeat at Norwich, April 1987.

This thing about Kenny being sullen is rubbish. He's got a great sense of humour, as anyone who played with him will tell you. If he appears uncommunicative, it's just that he's understandably wary about certain newspapers.
Alan Hansen, 1992.

He's incredibly intense about football. He's the only person I've ever seen come off during a match who's still playing every ball. Normally when players are substituted, you'll see them in the dug-out winding down. Kenny still kicks and heads everything.
Alan Hansen, 1992.

ENGLAND

The [English] Football League was the creation of one William McGregor, a Perthshire draper who bought a shop in Birmingham near the Aston Villa ground. McGregor joined Villa, although not for athletic purposes, as he later admitted when he revealed he had only ever played football on a single, unsuccessful occasion: 'I tried it once when I was very young and had to take to bed for a week.'
Roddy Forsyth, *The Only Game*, 1990.

An Englishman with footballing talent often became a stranger in his own land . . . The Liverpool side which played the club's first-ever league game in September 1893 with ten Scotsmen and a goalkeeper called McOwen . . . was a significant advance from an English point of view, because the very first Liverpool team, seen in a friendly against Rotherham, consisted of 11 Scots.
Roddy Forsyth, *The Only Game*, 1990.

The first [English] league goal was scored by Jack Gordon (nationality inevitable), a member of the Preston North End team known as the Invincibles.
Roddy Forsyth, *The Only Game*, 1990.

There's a strong sense that we should do England every time we meet them and I certainly love doing that.
SFA secretary **Ernie Walker**, *Only a Game?*, BBC documentary, 1985.

We hate you, really. No holds barred. 'Cause I know the same applies. I've seen it in dressing-rooms with Scottish and English players.
Bobby Robson, *Only a Game?*, BBC documentary, 1985.

After we beat England at Hampden Billy [McNeill] nicked the ball and we went up to Arden where John Colrain lived. We were going to a little party up there and we were out in the street with the ball at two in the morning, kicking it up and down the street, me and Jimmy and Mick Jackson, Billy

McNeill, John Colrain. In the afternoon there was 130,000 at Hampden and there we were kicking it about in the street.
Pat Crerand recalls the 1962 win over England, *Only a Game?*, BBC documentary, 1985.

If it had been 3–1 instead of 2–1 and there had only been a minute to go, I wanted to score an own goal to make it a hat-trick. Bill Brown says, 'You're not on.' Just for a laugh. That'd have been good, wouldn't it?
Jim Baxter recalls scoring two goals in the 1963 Wembley win, *Only a Game?*, BBC documentary, 1985.

My philosophy was, it was worth all the effort, put everything in, think of nothing else, do your proper planning, because it made life that little bit easier in the dressing-room for the rest of the season.
Bobby Charlton on the importance of beating Scotland, *Only a Game?*, BBC documentary, 1985.

When we won the semi-final of the European Cup, I remember Kenneth Wolstenholme saying: 'We've made it!' We became British that night, I don't mind that because I like to see the British game being successful, but I'd prefer to see the Scottish game successful.
Jock Stein recalling 1967.

If anyone asked me, of all the world teams that were going to come to Wembley [and win] the year after you'd won the World Cup, I'd have said the most likely to do that would've been the Scots.
Bobby Charlton, *Only a Game?*, BBC documentary, 1985.

Wee [Alan] Ball was running about, he was the hero of the World Cup and Bremner says, 'Call him Jimmy Clitheroe,' – you know, the comic with the short trousers and the squeaky voice? So I kept calling him 'Jimmy Clitheroe' and trying to nutmeg him and all that. Oh, he was goin' hairy.
Jim Baxter on Scotland's 1967 win at Wembley, *Only a Game?*, BBC documentary, 1985.

Denis [Law] and I went down to the bar in the Café Royal after the game. It was like Wembley all over again. There was this

table with twelve of them sitting round it, the Wembley turf on it. The kitty in the middle and all the drinks round about it. They'd all pinched a bit of turf. This is in the Café Royal.
Baxter on 1967, *Only a Game?*, BBC documentary, 1985.

Piccadilly Circus after Wembley – you can imagine it, thronging with people. I looked out of the car window at some traffic lights and who's standing there but my dad and my uncle. I rolled down the window – I'd Denis Law, John Greig and a few others in the car – and says, 'Dad, jump in, we're going to a party.' And my dad, in his right Fife accent, says, 'Ah, it's awright son, me and yer Uncle Jock'll just go to the pictures!'
Baxter on 1967, *Only a Game?*, BBC documentary, 1985.

I remember getting off the bus one day, about '71 or '72, with Alan Ball. Alan and myself were England fanatics, right . . . Just as we're getting off, a Scots lad with a kilt ran up and butted the bus! I can imagine him going back to his mates and saying, 'I really stuck it on them!'
Emlyn Hughes, *Only a Game?*, BBC documentary, 1985.

I absolutely loved playing against Scotland, the same way I loved playing for Liverpool against Everton. I always used to get stick, but I took that as a compliment. In fact, a Scots fella once said to me, 'You could be Scottish.' I took it to mean I got stuck in and showed emotion like the Scots.
Emlyn Hughes, April 1987.

We got beat 2–0 and I was embarrassed to come off the pitch. He [Jimmy Johnstone] absolutely crucified me. Alf Ramsey came up and he said, 'You've just played against a world-class player today. He can do that to anybody.'
Emlyn Hughes, *Only a Game?*, BBC documentary, 1985.

Bags of rubbish were piled up everywhere. The wind was blowing litter this way and that. I wondered what I'd let myself in for. I drove straight past the ground in this dismayed state, not knowing that the Parkhead stand, complete with wire mesh-covered windows, was also the front entrance. I'd imagined at first sight it must be Barlinnie Prison.
Celtic keeper **Peter Latchford**, 1978, recalling his February 1975 transfer from West Brom.

I knew as soon as I heard Jimmy Hill describe Narey's strike as a 'toe-poke' that it would not be taken lying down by our people. It was to be construed as some monstrous cultural insult, like calling the Clyde-built *Queen Elizabeth* a paddle-steamer . . . [Hill] was certainly no studio wallflower. He loved the attention of the Scottish supporters forever after. On match days . . . no man could have been prouder of being singled out for mob abuse. The 'Jimmy Hill's a Poof' banner frequently seen amongst Scottish fans was not only singularly inaccurate but was to Jimmy simply an eccentric sign of endearment.
Archie MacPherson, *Action Replays*, 1991.

The Aussies, they were fighting for us, the New Zealanders. I have nothing against them. I love 'em, same as the Scots. Just the same in my book. So it is rather strange that they look upon me as some sort of tribal totem pole to stick pins in.
Jimmy Hill, *Only a Game?*, BBC documentary, 1985.

That's the way the game is in England. A lot of very average players getting paid high salaries and just being professional.
Charlie Nicholas, *Only a Game?*, BBC documentary, 1985.

I'd been approached by Manchester United, and Spurs were interested, but the way the supporters came up to me and said, 'Are you going to sign?' and 'It's great to have you with us, big man', I thought, 'Bloody hell, this is a mega club, this is the big time.'
Terry Butcher on joining Rangers.

I was seven years old when I watched Ramsey lead England to their win over West Germany in 1966. Then people didn't realise the scale of what he had done. If that happened now, the man in charge would become the most popular figure of the 20th century in England.
Ayr boss **Simon Stainrod**, January 1994.

I said he was mistaken, that it wasn't so great because it had happened before. This man said that Liverpool was definitely the first city to do it [have two clubs in the finals of two European competitions]. I said, 'No, it happened in this country, it happened in Scotland. Rangers lost in the Cup-Winners' Cup final the year we won the European Cup.' It's

how you see it. It angers you. I was watching [President] Reagan the other day and he said, 'We have great relationships with England and Germany now.' I think it's incredible when we bring them up on these things – particularly the English – they all say we're small-minded but they would never be classed as tied to Scotland.
Jock Stein, 1985.

CHAIRMEN OF THE BOARD

The ideal board of directors should be made up of three men – two dead and the other dying.
Tommy Docherty, 1977.

If I had to spend ten years in gaol and had to choose a companion, I'd choose Doc. He'd make it seem like one year.
Rotherham chairman **Eric Purshouse**, *Call The Doc*, 1981.

'Well, Tom,' he [Jim Gregory, QPR chairman] said, 'I'm thinking of calling it a day.' Tongue-in-cheek, I replied: 'I wouldn't do that, chairman, I think you're doing a good job.'
Tommy Docherty, *Call the Doc*,1981.

In some ways we're all a little mad because there must be easier ways to earn a living.
Hearts chairman **Wallace Mercer**, *Only a Game?*, BBC documentary, 1985.

People are very conservative, even in Glasgow. By and large we're not very receptive of good ideas or what they think are revolutionary ideas. Change is something to be resisted.
Aberdeen director **Chris Anderson**, *Only a Game?*, BBC documentary, 1985.

I very much doubt if I could approach life in the manner he does. He's on sticks, he's never in a chair. It's an inconvenience to him and that's all it is. He's larger than life.
Graeme Souness on David Murray, November 1990.

Celtic have spent £4.5 million on new players in the last few years, and that's a bloody big biscuit tin.
Celtic chief executive **Terry Cassidy**, January 1991. (The biscuit tin was a reference to Celtic's cash problems.)

My first job has been to go round the place and ask people what they actually do. Some of them could not tell me.
Terry Cassidy, January 1991.

Their cash was only a small percentage of our income.
Terry Cassidy, after Parkhead box-holders withdrew their support after
Cassidy had referred to them as 'fair-weather supporters', 1991.

Do you recall Jack McGinn being interviewed on *Scotsport*
about the proposals to build a new stadium for Celtic? When
he was asked the quite reasonable question about where Celtic
were going to come up with the £30-odd million in readies
required to finance such a project, he was particularly evasive,
mumbling something about not wanting to discuss that in case
other people got to hear of it. The viewer was left with the
clear impression that Jack, Jimmy Farrell and Chris White (the
Paradise Gang) were going to rob a bank.
Alastiar McSporran, *The Absolute Game* fanzine, April 1991.

We were quite keen to see the impact of having no sponsor on
the shirt. Personally I think it looks a lot better without one.
Celtic vice-chairman **David Smith** explaining why Celtic had no jersey
sponsor, December 1992.

Are you sure he was being serious?
Celtic director **Michael Kelly**, when Smith's remark was quoted to him.

I was advised that David Holmes was an experienced footballing man when he was made vice-chairman. He turned out to
be a disaster for the club.
Dundee chairman **Ron Dixon**, August 1993.

Every decision regarding the playing side is Walter's. He may
ask me to handle some of the financial negotiations, but that is
all. I have never interfered, ever, in a transfer. Walter could
even have blocked the Trevor Steven sale at any time. If I ever
interfere I know who he can blame if anything goes wrong.
Rangers chairman **David Murray**, 1993.

There are 35,000 Celtic fans who can see what this team needs
on the park. I surely do not have to tell seven directors what
that is, do I?
Lou Macari, January 1994.

I pleaded with him not to order a parrot in the first place. Celtic weren't doing particularly well at the time and I thought a Scottish lion might be more appropriate.

Novelty promotions company boss Janie Bacon, after lodging a claim against Celtic director **Michael Kelly**, who had allegedly deducted £100 from the bill for a parrot costume hired for a Parkhead photocall, February 1994.

We [Chelsea] travelled to Baghdad to play the Iraqi national side and to allow our chairman Ken Bates to meet his soulmate Saddam Hussein (only kidding, Ken, old pal).

Pat Nevin, February 1994.

MANAGEMENT

I love football but I positively hate being a manager.
West Ham boss **Lou Macari**, 1989.

I've heard it said you can't be a football manager and tell the truth. Well, I'm going to have a go at it.
Liam Brady on being appointed Celtic boss, 1991.

When people tell me that fans want style and entertainment first I don't believe it. Fans want to win. Style's a bonus.
Birmingham manager **Lou Macari**, 1991.

Somebody said to me early in my career, 'Do you not think you're a wee bit hard on them?' I said, 'No, no way.' I am hard on them because I decided they'll know exactly what I'm thinking. You must be 100 per cent honest and that's the part players don't like.
Jim McLean, *Only a Game?*, BBC documentary, 1985.

If I ask the players for less than perfection they'll definitely give me less.
Jim McLean, *Only a Game?*, BBC documentary, 1985.

People say I moan and groan, but if you are to get anywhere or achieve anything you need consistency. I know what our players are capable of. If you settle for less, you get less.
Motherwell manager **Tommy McLean**, December 1993. Motherwell were joint top of the Premier League at the time.

He managed with a velvet glove. A kind man, generous man, beautiful man. But everyone at Old Trafford knew who was the manager.
Bobby Robson on Matt Busby, *Only a Game?*, BBC documentary, 1985.

If I was playing particularly badly I couldn't get him out of my mind. I thought, 'He's not going to be happy with this.'
Bobby Charlton on Matt Busby, *Only a Game?*, BBC documentary, 1985.

The great thing about Busby was that you would go in there fighting and full of demands. And he would give you nothing at all. He might even take a tenner off your wages. And you would come out thinking, 'What a great guy.' I remember going in there once absolutely livid. And ten minutes later I came out, no better off, walking on air. Delighted.

Eamon Dunphy on Matt Busby, *Only a Game?*, BBC documentary, 1985.

They were on £300 a week, the lowest-paid players in the First Division. Shilton wanted £400 a week. End of deal. When I signed Jimmy Greenhoff from Stoke in 1976 he took a £50-a-week pay cut to come to United.

Tommy Docherty, recalling Matt Busby's prudent use of money. (Quoted in *A Strange Kind of Glory* by Eamon Dunphy, 1991.)

At the time, I'd a good offer to go to England and I talked it over with the chairman of Celtic and he said, out of the blue, 'How would you like to come back?' I didn't think it would work because Celtic had never worked with a manager having a full say. But I was assured I'd be given full control of the side.

Jock Stein, *Only a Game?*, BBC documentary, 1985.

I don't have enough time to be a manager.

Gregor Abel, quitting as Falkirk manager, February 1984.

There is no way I could have gone and managed, with all due respect, any of the English Third and Fourth Division teams and have had the same enthusiasm as I've had in the past for football. Managing Rangers has to be put in the same bracket as managing Manchester United.

Graeme Souness, September 1986.

As someone who over the last ten years has been used to humping marker cones, dirty jerseys and the like, I find this up-front bit a touch worrying. I was at Oldham the other week and kids who had seen my picture in the papers were asking for my autograph. It was a bit embarrassing.

Andy Roxburgh shortly after being appointed Scotland coach, September 1986.

He stood there belting the living daylights out of this tree and inviting us to join him. It had soft bark which didn't hurt your fists. The manager was right. He obviously knew something about trees.

Colin Walsh of Nottingham Forest revealing Brian Clough's arcane forestry knowledge in Graz, Austria. (Quoted in *Clough – A Biography* by Tony Francis, 1987.)

Perhaps managers should reflect upon whether immediately after a game is the proper time to comment on events during it.

SFA secretary designate **Jim Farry**, January 1990.

I can cope with football but one thing I can't cope with is treachery, and that's what I had at Swindon.

Birmingham boss **Lou Macari**, February 1991.

From Monday to Friday a manager's job is superb. It's the other bit that can be a problem.

Alex MacDonald after being sacked by Hearts, 1991.

There was about an hour, just of Shankly talking, and while some of it was, well, piffle, other bits were unbelievably profound. Being young, we just wanted to hear music and tried to lose the tapes. But Fergie made us listen. I'm sure he could recite them verbatim. Funnily enough, I've got a set of the tapes myself now.

Reading boss **Mark McGhee** recalling the tapes on the Aberdeen team bus, January 1994.

Today we're lucky in football management, there are rewards and benefits, and I'm aware of what I've got while there are people in our country who are unemployed. But the stress can accompany me. Sometimes I'm lying on a beach in the summer and the only thing going through my head is football, Rangers, and who I should buy and who I should sell. It's an all-consuming thing.

Walter Smith, October 1993.

One player who left told me his new manager had charisma. I asked where he got it from and he replied: 'He made me captain.'

Scotland coach **Craig Brown**, October 1993.

I'd advise anyone to play as long as possible, even if it's only in the park on a Sunday afternoon. That is the best game. Managing is a poor second.
Liverpool manager **Graeme Souness**, 1992.

I couldn't say there is one correct style of management, it depends on your personality. Graeme [Souness] was loath to show the other side of himself in public. He preferred the aggressive image. Me, my first inclination is to get on with people. I think a confrontational edge tends to show a lack of confidence in a person.
Walter Smith, October 1993.

Even in the bad times, Jimmy [Sirrell], who was a bit of an eccentric character, could be humorous. I remember we arrived at the training ground in a fleet of cars but the manager was nowhere to be seen. Half an hour later he arrived, in the passenger seat of a friend's car, and duly apologised for being late. Jimmy explained that he had been in an accident and then suddenly pointed at Simon Stainrod, saying: 'And it was all your fucking fault.' Young Simon, who later moved to Queen's Park Rangers, Aston Villa and Stoke City, naturally looked bewildered as Jimmy continued his monologue. 'I'm driving along thinking about where to play Simon on Saturday,' he added. 'Will I use him right up front or coming forward from the midfield? Of course, being so lost in thought I drove through a red light and crashed into another car.'
Jimmy Johnstone, *Jinky – Now and Then.*

I always say I'll get over it when I grow up but there are no signs of it happening yet. I still find it impossible to drive past any sort of match. I've got to stop and watch it.
Scotland assistant boss **Craig Brown**, 1988.

Something happened to football in the mid-1970s. Suddenly managers became more important than players. Every magazine you picked up had Brian Clough, Ron Atkinson or Tommy Docherty inside. I don't believe in the cult of management and I don't want to add to it.
Andy Roxburgh, 1990.

You can hear what they're saying. The art is in pretending you can't. You've enough problems out there as it is.
Alan Hansen on advice from the dug-out, April 1993.

I bluffed it. I waved my hands and stuck out my chest like big Billy McNeill.
Reading boss **Mark McGhee** on his early managerial techniques, January 1994.

When I was at Celtic I was said to be a players' man and maybe that was true. In those days if the ship was sinking I would have thrown all 11 lifebelts to the players. Now I would keep one for myself, throw ten and lose a player.
St Mirren manager **David Hay** on the lessons of his sacking by Celtic, 1991.

I'm a great believer in getting the tackles in. After team talks Andy [Roxburgh] always asked, 'Anything to add, Broon?' And I'd say: 'Well, I've seen this lot and [rams fist into palm]. . .' I wasn't a gifted player, but I was an aggressive wee guy.
Scotland coach **Craig Brown**, October 1993.

Craig always used to say, 'Don't mistake kindness for softness.' That's a good description of his way of working. I remember one of our players had been sent off and Craig said to him, 'Tell me, son, is your father a joiner?' When the lad said no, Craig shot back, 'Well, who made your head then?'
Former Clyde striker **Robert Reilly** on Craig Brown, September 1993.

I was born in 1950, the Chinese Year of the Tiger. My personality reflects that.
Dundee United boss **Ivan Golac**, September 1993.

I was up at Old Trafford not long ago and sat in Fergie's seat in that sort of podium thing he's had built overlooking the pitch, and I thought, 'This is for me.'
Reading boss **Mark McGhee**, January 1994.

When they bury me I want one word only on my gravestone: 'Teacher'.
Andy Roxburgh, September 1986.

We all end up yesterday's men in this business. You're very quickly forgotten.
Jock Stein.

SOUNESS

Being successful has always been more important to me than being popular.
First line of **Graeme Souness's** autobiography, *No Half Measures*, 1985.

He was impatient, arrogant and tended to be flash; he wanted success and he wanted it yesterday.
Pat Welton, Spurs youth team coach to the 15-year-old Graeme Souness.

A rather moody young man . . . sullen yet aggressive, with enormous chips on his shoulder, convinced the world was against him.
Journalist **Hunter Davies** on the young Souness, *Souness of Sampdoria*.

I was totally wrong, it was immature, pure arrogance. I was 17 and thought I had a God-given right to be in Spurs' first team. At that time their midfield was Peters, Mullery and Perryman and I simply wasn't good enough. But I was young and Scottish and I thought I was the greatest. Spurs did me a favour. I left with a chip on my shoulder and a point to prove.
Graeme Souness, 1989.

There was a free holiday as the first prize. I was in there trying to win. It wasn't vanity. It was a free holiday I was after.
Souness recalling winning the Body Beautiful competition as a 12-year-old at Butlin's in Ayr, 1989.

The chocolate soldier. If Souness was chocolate he'd eat himself.
Archie Gemmill.

Archie was 90 per cent right. There was a lot of truth in what he said. We are going back to 1978, maybe I was a bit vain and thought the world revolved around me, but it was my way of motivating myself and it worked with Archie Gemmill. Every time I played against him after that I kicked him up in the air.
Souness, 1989.

SCOTTISH FOOTBALL QUOTATIONS

His mother used to say that anywhere he went trouble would follow pretty quickly.
Walter Smith on Graeme Souness, September 1991.

It was a watertight case. But I don't think Graeme and his family wanted any more of the publicity the issue had created.
West Lothian MP **Tam Dalyell** after raising Souness's case in the House of Commons, June 1971. The 17-year-old Souness had been out of football for six months after walking out on Spurs.

I had a big problem with Graeme when I took over . . . I had to get it through to him that if he did not screw the nut he'd be a bum for the rest of his life.
Middlesbrough boss **Jack Charlton**.

How could you be a playboy in Middlesbrough?
Souness, denying his 'Champagne Charlie' reputation, 1981.

It's very hard in England to keep up the macho footballer image if you have to go around the streets shouting 'Cuddles'.
Graeme Souness, 1982. (Cuddles was the Souness's Yorkshire Terrier.)

When that wall collapsed at Walsall as Liverpool scored their second goal, the video recording of the game shows Graeme Souness hurtling deep and immediately into the crowd to rescue and reassure while all around him people were still celebrating the goal.
Playwright **Alan Bleasdale**, Foreword to Souness's autobiography, 1985.

I have sometimes wished I could have played for England instead . . . From a purely financial point of view the rewards for being an England international footballer are far greater than for being a Jock.
Graeme Souness, *No Half Measures*, 1985.

I'm a professional footballer who plays for money. I've always been open about that. I can earn a great deal more by playing outside Scotland than I could in Scotland. But I'd still like to be player-manager of Rangers one day. I'd settle for manager . . . Anybody in their right mind, whether they be Welsh, Irish, Scottish or English would come back and manage Rangers. If they did anything at all they'd match Manchester United. It

would be nice to win the European Cup being manager of Rangers, wouldn't it?
Graeme Souness, September 1985.

I was involved in an incident when the youngsters who always hung around for autographs and photographs were pestering Kenny Dalglish. There was no chance of getting any rest at all and Gordon McQueen came into our room to see what all the noise and fuss was about. We decided to have a little game for the kids and grouped them together as if for a photograph before dousing them with water. It was a bit of fun and even the kids laughed but that was not how the incident was reported.
Graeme Souness, *No Half Measures*, 1985.

Graeme Souness doesn't intimidate or scare me. He's just another manager – one who has yet to prove himself at managerial level.
Falkirk's **Billy Lamont**, after taking a team to promotion for the third time in six seasons, August 1986.

The reaction from the boss was typical Souness. He was chuffed to bits that, in his first game, his players had shown such team spirit. He always said that in Italy players would walk away saying, 'It's up to you, mate.' So he loved the fact we were all in it together.
Ex-Ranger **Stuart Munro**, January 1994, on Souness's debut against Hibs in August 1986. Souness was sent off and both sides were later fined after a centre-circle brawl.

We have to expect intimidation and I am the one who was suckered into it.
Graeme Souness on being sent off on his Rangers debut in August 1986.

I've never been more depressed than the time I was sent off against Hibs. It was the first game of the season. I was brought up in Albert Street near the Hibs ground, my whole family came from that area, my dad used to sneak into the ground at night to play football on the grass at Easter Road, and I got sent off in my own backyard. I remember seeing the red card and looking up, there were 30,000 people jeering and I could see my dad in the front row of the director's box. I can still feel the shame now. I know it sounds like Hollywood, but I've never felt so alone. I'd let my dad down, humiliated him in his own street. That was my lowest moment in football. I just sat in the dressing-room with my head in my hands hating myself for what I'd done.

Graeme Souness, 1989.

Rangers Football Club and Mr Souness have accepted full responsibility for their part in the misbehaviour and have apologised unreservedly to the Association. Nevertheless, the Association wishes to make it clear behaviour of the type witnessed on 9 August will not be tolerated in the Scottish game. The committee accordingly decided Rangers Football Club will be fined the sum of £5000 and Mr Souness will be suspended for a further three matches from Thursday, 21 August.

SFA statement after Souness's Rangers debut, August 1986.

How Davie Dodds went through the game without being spoken to, booked, or sent off is beyond me. He uses his hands so often he's more suited to volleyball. Every time Richard Gough or Terry Butcher went for a high ball they were heading his elbows.

Graeme Souness on the Aberdeen striker after a bad-tempered game at Pittodrie, 1988. Within a year Souness had signed Dodds for Rangers.

I have the feeling he is being singled out for harsher treatment than others by referees.

Rangers assistant boss **Walter Smith** after Graeme Souness was sent off – for the third time in a year – against Celtic, August 1987.

I am not interested in critics of Rangers.

Graeme Souness, *A Manager's Diary*, 1989.

It may be good in life to think the world's against you. You fight harder.

Graeme Souness, 1989.

Would you leave your home like that?

St Johnstone tea-lady **Aggie Moffat** to Souness after the Rangers manager allegedly tipped over a tea urn in the dressing-room, 1990.

When I came back, I told Souness I was staying put. That's when he threw the Rothman's Football Yearbook at me and said, 'Find yourself a club in there.'
Ibrox cult figure **Scott Nisbet**, January 1993, recalling turning down a 1990 move to Dundee.

Graeme is not one to keep his emotions to himself. He wears his heart on his sleeve, throws a few pies and television sets about and you know exactly where you are with him.
Terry Butcher.

His body is absolutely beautiful. He was never off the massage table. I used to spend an hour a day on him.
Scotland physio **Jimmy Steele** on Graeme Souness, 1990.

I've thought long and hard about why things went wrong with us. There was no particular incident, just a gradual feeling that I was taking more than my fair share of stick in dressing-room post-mortems. I was forever being compared unfavourably to Ian Rush. I don't think he ever forgave me for not being a Rushie clone. I was told I wasn't as mentally alert as Rush. I didn't work as hard as him. I didn't finish as well as him, and so on . . . So there was friction between us, perhaps not right at the start, but certainly fairly early into our relationship. Looking back, I was probably my own worst enemy. Others would take a tongue-lashing in silence – I would answer back.
Ally McCoist on Graeme Souness, *Ally McCoist – My Story*

It wasn't a case of my coming back to show these naive Scotsmen how it's all done. But the thing I have found here, and I have found hard to handle, is that there is a fair bit of bitterness and jealousy, bordering on hatred, from people within the game towards this club. I think I increased that hatred and I admit I should have handled myself better. But there were a few people trying to make their mark. I would respond with no worse a tackle, then get booked or sent off. I felt I was set up slightly.
Souness, November 1990.

I know that from the first day I took this job at Ibrox there have been those who have said I was merely using Rangers as a stepping-stone to so-called bigger things in England.
Graeme Souness, 1988.

The only way I'll leave Rangers is if I'm sacked.
Graeme Souness, 1989.

Even going back to Liverpool would be a downward step.
Graeme Souness, September 1986.

I'd be very flattered to be offered the Liverpool job but I would never contemplate leaving Ibrox.
Souness, 18 February 1991. By April he had succeeded Kenny Dalglish at Anfield.

I've no intention of ever leaving this place [Ibrox]. I see my short-term and my long-term future here. I'm very fortunate to work with some great people and we are building something that will last a very long time.
Graeme Souness, two months before leaving Rangers for Liverpool, 1991.

I've gone as far as I'll be allowed to go to achieve success at this football club.
Souness quits Ibrox, 16 April 1991.

He [Souness] and I have little rituals. We dine together on Friday nights, chat in the manager's office before games and find time for a few words of reflection afterwards. On the Friday before he broke the news to me, we had dinner at Cosmo's in Edinburgh as normal, then chatted before the Hibs game at Ibrox. But afterwards he was off like a shot. On Sundays we always speak. There was no call. On Mondays we always speak. Nothing. On Monday night we had dinner at the Marché Noir in Edinburgh but things were not right. Next night it all clicked. On Saturdays we always have the rituals of saying, 'See you later'. It's something we always say. But that Saturday, Graeme hadn't said it. I knew that was it.
David Murray, April 1991.

When Graeme left, the day his resignation was announced he drove to Liverpool in a six-week-old silver Mercedes 300SL worth £60,000. He still has that car. We have asked Liverpool to make us an offer for it.
Rangers chairman **David Murray**, April 1991.

When I was at Spurs I was always a Middlesbrough fan who'd always supported Liverpool, and the only team I would have moved to Italy for would have been Sampdoria because when I was a boy I used to skip school in Edinburgh and sneak into Italy to watch them. But as I stood there cheering on Sampdoria I couldn't forget that as a foetus I was an avid Rangers fan.

'Graeme Souness', BBC Radio spoof documentary, *Only an Excuse*, 1986.

Graeme and I never fell out because I'd say to him, 'Graeme, let's speak tomorrow, let's not fall out', and that's what we've always done . . . we'll still remain friends. [His departure] was the best thing that happened to Rangers, but not necessarily the best thing for Graeme. Graeme was needed to turn the big ship round. It was heading for the rocks. But I don't think we needed that abrasive attitude, falling out with people, on a regular basis.

David Murray, 1993.

Anybody who plays for me should be a bad loser.

Graeme Souness, shortly after losing the English title to Arsenal, 1991.

Souness could have played for any country in the world.

Bobby Robson, 1985.

I remember the incident well. To me, it sums up the man. We were murdering a Finnish side in the UEFA Cup, and as he passed me, this cocky 17-year-old scowled and said, 'About bloody time. I should have been on ages ago.'

Former Spurs midfielder **Alan Mullery**, on Souness's only appearance for the London club, September 1986.

BIG JOCK (1)

He doesn't fill your head with wee motors.
Bobby Lennox on Jock Stein.

Down there for eight hours you're away from God's fresh air and sunshine and there's nothing that can compensate for that. There's nothing as dark as the darkness down a pit, the blackness that closes in on you if your lamp goes out. You'd think you would see some kind of shapes but you can see nothing, nothing but the inside of your head. I think everybody should go down the pit at least once to learn what darkness is.
Jock Stein, quoted in Hugh McIlvanney's obituary of him, *The Observer*, 15 September 1985.

He gave me the best piece of advice I ever got – that it's what you do away from the park that determines your level of fitness on it. So I took up hunting, shooting and fishing and got myself well away from smoky cities.
Tommy Gemmell, August 1978.

I once watched a match with him in Madrid before Celtic played Atletico Madrid. It was interesting the way he worked out how teams were going to play. He had a blank sheet of paper and he'd just go across it where the ball was. So at the end of 90 minutes you have this great scrawl, but what you could see was where the ball went and who got the ball most.
Journalist **Ian Archer** on Stein, *Only a Game?*, BBC documentary, 1985.

The problem for us is that Big Jock and his players spoiled it for everyone who came after them.
Celtic boss **Lou Macari**, January 1994.

I can remember him telling me at half-time [in a match against Wales in 1985] that I would be coming off in the second-half, allowing Davie Cooper to go on. That was how he wanted to play it and I was ready to argue a little bit when Fergie, who was assistant manager at the time, said to me: 'Leave it alone. He's not well. Just leave it.'

Gordon Strachan, *Strachan Style*, 1991. Stein suffered a fatal heart attack shortly after the match ended.

Bob Paisley was brilliant but he could not always communicate with the players. Joe Fagan had technical knowledge and could communicate but he got the job when, maybe, he was too old for it. Jock had everything. He had the knowledge; he had that nasty bit that managers must have; and he could communicate. On top of it all, he was six feet tall, and sometimes he seemed to get bigger as he was talking to you. He was the best.

Graeme Souness in *Jock Stein; The Authorised Biography*, 1988.

BIG JOCK (2)

In those days in pre-season training you were eased in relatively gently. Not for Jock. The first session he had the 40 of us out there and we ran round the track for 40 minutes. You jogged, you never walked, you had 40 minutes non-stop running – then you were up and down the old, big terracings. It was the hardest training session I've ever experienced. There was only six people left at the end of it. The rest were bedraggled all the way round the track. Some of them actually needed oxygen. It was ferocious.

Sandy Jardine on the Wallace training methods, 1993.

I thought he was mad. We hadn't training anything like the way Jock made us train. But his training helped me play to the age of 36.

John Greig on Wallace.

There's a hill there and you'll never see anything like it in your life. We used to see Lawrence of Arabia's bones there. Big Jock used to say, 'If you're going to be sick, put your head to one side and be sick – but keep running.' You weren't allowed to stop.

Derek Johnstone remembering the sands of Gullane.

JOLLY JIM

Every morning in life I arrive at Tannadice and start switching off lights in the place . . . Good housekeeping is the secret at Tannadice.
Jim McLean, *Jousting With Giants*.

The players will receive only two-thirds of the extra bonus they were on for entertaining, despite winning 6–1. There was some slackness and mistakes.
Jim McLean after beating Motherwell, March 1981.

Against Motherwell I was supposed to have fined the players for lack of entertainment after they had scored five goals in the first half in the Scottish Cup tie at Tannadice. Eventually we won the game 6–1 but there were times when we were sluggish, times when we might have thrown the game away and gone out of the Cup. I wasn't happy with that and I docked the players a special bonus payment which was on offer then if they produced an exceptional performance. Against smaller teams we often have them on a win bonus and this extra £50 if the display they give is a very special one. Although we won 6–1 I didn't think they merited that extra payment.
Jim McLean, *Jousting With Giants*.

He put a lot of mediocre players on the gravy train. But for him they would be nothing more than names on a programme.
Andy Gray on Jim McLean, April 1987.

I have been a director for 33 years and we are plunged into the biggest crisis in my time here because of the referee committee's action yesterday.
Dundee United chairman **George Fox**, after Jim McLean tendered his resignation, 8 July 1988, after being fined £4000 by the SFA and banned from the dug-out for three years after a confrontation with Aberdeen skipper Willie Miller during a Scottish Cup semi-final replay in April 1988.

If I fall out with Alex Smith, who is an old friend of mine, I'll only have my wife left to talk to and she sometimes doesn't talk back to me.
Jim McLean, February 1989.

Tannadice just did not seem the same without Wee Jim sitting there, savaging his players and griping over some tactical malfunction which had plainly ruined his whole weekend.
Journalist **Jack Sawkins**, *Sunday Times*, November 1989.

He has a psychic ability to discern the profile of the complete footballer disguised within the gangly frame of a half-formed adolescent.
Journalist **Roddy Forsyth** on McLean, *The Only Game*, 1990.

I like him. We have had our differences – Jim always needs to be given the credit for everything and I was furious when he demanded £50,000 before I was allowed to go to Ibrox – but you cannot argue with his record.
Walter Smith on Jim McLean, September 1991.

I no longer intend to be at press conferences because managers are muzzled by the SFA from speaking about important issues which happen in games. Fans deserve to hear what clubs feel about incidents, but that is not possible and as far as I am concerned that makes it a waste of time attending conferences. The SFA secretary [Jim Farry] was highly critical of managers recently and appears to be allowed freedom of speech while preventing us.
Jim McLean, October 1991.

I won't say I'm superstitious about rituals but you should see the route we take when we go to Edinburgh.
Jim McLean, 1992.

I admire the guy, but I like him as well. Okay, he doesn't have a Mr Bobbysox personality. He can be a rather prickly natured fellow. But what do people want? Bob Hope *and* a good football team? What he's done for that club is immeasurable. I've been over there when he's been putting screws in doors and vacuuming the carpets. He's done every filthy job there is to get them where they are today and I bet he hasn't had three

people slap him on the back and say, 'Well done'. If I was a Dundee United fan I'd remember him in my prayers every single day – God bless Jim McLean, keep him healthy.
Dundee chairman **Ron Dixon**, August 1993.

He [Jim McLean] is quick-tempered and his behaviour can be erratic and unpredictable.
Sheriff **Graham Cox**, during a civil hearing involving former Dundee United assistant manager Steve Murray.

FERGIE

My father worked in the shipyards, my brother worked in the shipyards, and my uncles worked in the shipyards. At one time the population of Govan was 90,000 people. I was down at that famous Boys Club, Harmony Row, and the lad that runs that, Bob Innes, he's been there for 40 years and now he's working out of an old church, trying to send some young boys on their merry way.
Alex Ferguson, *Only a Game?*, BBC documentary, 1985.

When I was a boy it wasn't, were you going to get a job, it was, what were you going to work at? You had a choice.
Alex Ferguson, *Only a Game?*, BBC documentary, 1985.

There's nothing wrong with losing your temper. They get plenty praise. There's times when it's suitable to lose your temper.
Alex Ferguson on players, *Only a Game?*, BBC documentary, 1985.

The Prime Minister must be delighted. Rangers have even managed to keep her out of the news.
Aberdeen boss **Alex Ferguson**, August 1986.

I was happy that he had got the job he wanted. He had told me after the World Cup in Mexico that it was the job he wanted most – one of two jobs which would tempt him away from Aberdeen, the other being Barcelona.
Gordon Strachan on Ferguson getting the Manchester United job, *Strachan Style*, 1991.

You can't go into a club and tell people their fitness is terrible, that they're bevvying, they're playing too much golf, and their ground is filthy. You simply have to improve things bit by bit.
Manchester United boss **Alex Ferguson**, December 1986.

We went to Liverpool, attacked them, thought we were the better team, and were 3–0 down at half-time. You stand in the dressing-room and think, 'This isn't fair'.
Alex Ferguson after losing 4–0 at Anfield, 1990.

I never thought I'd see the day when I said we needed more Englishmen in our squad.
Alex Ferguson on UEFA'S restrictions on foreign players, 1991.

He's a complex character and even the people who get close to him will never really know him. They never get the chance. Players certainly don't get inside his head. He'll mingle with them one day and then the next he won't say a word.
Gordon Strachan on Alex Ferguson, October 1992.

Having players you've sold come back and score against you is what football is all about.
Alex Ferguson, 1992.

He kicks every ball, feels every tackle. He is a man who shows his emotions.
Kevin Moran on Alex Ferguson, 1993.

He was one for coming out with the strangest of things. A couple of Fergie-isms were: 'Have you ever seen a Pakistani funeral?' or 'Have you ever seen an Italian with a cold?' You would be left to ponder what he meant.
Pat Stanton, Ferguson's former assistant at Aberdeen, 1989.

They've obviously never been to a Glasgow wedding.
Alex Ferguson, October 1993, making light of the hostile atmosphere Manchester United could expect in Istanbul against Galatasaray.

Every manager has to start somewhere. After all, Alex Ferguson was once at East Stirling, although his team didn't have to change in a Portakabin.
Cowdenbeath boss **John Reilly**, December 1993.

The BBC are dying for us to lose. Everyone is from Liverpool with a Liverpool supporters' flag. They'll be here every time until we lose, that mob – Barry, Bob, Hansen, the lot of them, Liverpool Supporters Association.
Manchester United boss **Ferguson** after the BBC's Jimmy Hill had called Eric Cantona 'despicable' for kicking Norwich defender John Polston in an FA Cup tie, January 1994.

THE DOC SPEAKS

This player is going to make a great manager one day . . . But wherever he goes and whatever he does, they will certainly know he has been there.
Tom Finney, after the 1954 Preston v West Brom FA Cup final, quoted in *Call the Doc* by Tommy Docherty, 1981.

They offered me a handshake of £10,000 to settle amicably. I told them they would need to be a lot more amicable than that.
Tommy Docherty, after being sacked as manager of Preston, 1981.

I talk a lot. On any subject. Which is always football.
Tommy Docherty, 1970s.

I promised Rotherham I'd take them out of the Second Division. I did – into the Third Division.
Tommy Docherty, *Call the Doc*, 1981.

I told the Chelsea chairman he didn't want a coach – he wanted a hearse.
Tommy Docherty, *Call the Doc*, 1981.

The Doc was always too busy thinking up his next smart remark, so far as I could see, and he tended to let that obscure the managerial skills he possessed.
Danny McGrain, *In Sunshine or in Shadow*, 1987.

When I signed him [Jim Holton] from Shrewsbury for £100,000, Harry Gregg said, 'You've got a player who doesn't know the meaning of the word defeat.' A week later I phoned Harry back and said, 'Aye, and defeat's not the only word he doesn't know the meaning of. There's pass, control, dribble . . .'
Tommy Docherty.

He eats cheats for breakfast. He's the only manager who can hold a serious, face-to-face conversation and tell you what's happening 20 yards behind him.
Manchester United coach **Tommy Cavanagh**, quoted in *Call the Doc*, 1981.

THE DOC SPEAKS

He could start an argument in an empty house.
Jimmy Nicholl on the Doc.

Docherty tried to ruin me, my career and my family. I hate him.
Manchester United and Scotland international **Willie Morgan**.

After the match an official asked for two of my players to take a dope test. I offered him the referee.
Tommy Docherty after a 5–1 defeat by Brighton relegated Wolves to the Third Division, 1985.

It would be easier to find Howard Hughes and Martin Bormann than to find the people who run Wolves.
Tommy Docherty after being sacked as manager of Wolves, July 1985.

Whenever people criticise Tommy to my face I ask them if they either know him or have worked with him. When they say no my reply is 'All you know is what you read in the newspapers – he is the finest bloke I've ever worked with in the game.'
Neville Briggs, Stoke chief scout, quoted in *Call the Doc*, 1981.

How's the wife?
Tommy Docherty to Altrincham's 69-year-old physio, Jeff Warburton, 1987. (Docherty had lost his job as manager of Manchester United in 1977 after falling in love with the wife of United's physio, Laurie Brown.)

SHANKS

It's the greatest thing in the world, natural enthusiasm. You're nothing without it.
Bill Shankly, *Only a Game?*, BBC documentary, 1985.

When I told people in Scotland that England were coming up with a winger who was better than Matthews they all laughed at me. They weren't bloody laughing when big Geordie Young was running all over Hampden Park looking for Tommy Finney.
Bill Shankly.

He never had a day's illness. He never smoked. He never drank. He used to do all the training, five-a-sides, running, everything. He didn't want to appear weak in any way. He'd be running with you, laughing and joking with you. At the end of the training he'd walk in and say, 'You know something, boys? When I die, I want to be the fittest man ever to die.'
Emlyn Hughes on Shankly, *Only a Game?*, BBC documentary, 1985.

I was making a bee-line for Stanley Matthews, and as I got across he hooked it over my head and Tommy Lawton lashed it into the net with his head. I remember the noise the ball made, squishing against the wet net. And Lawton said, 'Get in!' I heard him saying this. The net was squishing with noise. Bloody awful, it was.
Bill Shankly recalling the April 1939 Scotland v England game, *Only a Game?*, BBC documentary, 1985.

He's a colossus. Come outside and I'll give you a walk round him.
Bill Shankly on Ron Yeats, his 6' 2", 14-stone signing from Dundee United, 1961.

With him at centre-half, we could play Arthur Askey in goal.
Shankly on Yeats, 1962.

He signed Alec Lindsay, who was a left-back, from Bury and the lad had two years in the reserves at Anfield until the day came for his debut. Shanks said to him, 'Now look, Alec, when you get the ball I want you to beat a couple of men and smash it into the back of the net the way you did at Bury.' Alec Lindsay says, 'But boss, that wasn't me, that was Bobby Kerr.' So Shanks turns to Bob Paisley and says, 'Christ, Bob, we've signed the wrong player!'
Tommy Docherty.

I had thousands of grievances with Shanks. But if you faced him, he said his point of view, you said yours, and you did what he said and it was over and done with.
Emlyn Hughes, *Only a Game?*, BBC documentary, 1985.

If you were injured he wouldn't talk to you. He took it personally. You didn't exist. You were no use to Liverpool Football Club.
Ian St John on Shankly.

The trouble with referees is that they know the rules but they don't know the game.
Shankly, 1971.

It's dead easy. I just get up and tell a few Bill Shankly stories.
Emlyn Hughes on the art of after-dinner speaking, February 1987.

THE OLD FIRM

Ancient Rome suffered from chariot hooligans. There were two main factions, the Greens and the Blues, and the rivalry between their supporters was intense. The hatred between them was heightened by the fact that they adhered to different religious beliefs, rather like the soccer clubs of [Catholic] Celtic and [Protestant] Rangers in Glasgow today. The worst riot in the history of sport occurred in January of the year 512, when fighting broke out between supporters of the Blues and Greens. It lasted several days and developed into a massacre in which at least 30,000 people lost their lives.
Desmond Morris, *The Soccer Tribe*, 1981.

Rampant bigotry, religious intolerance, vile suspicion and bitter, bitter hatred – yes, Scotland needs a strong Old Firm.
Only an Excuse '93 stage show.

In the famous 7–1 victory over Rangers in the 1957 League Cup final, a technician in London, tele-recording the match all the way down the line from Hampden, put a dust cover over the lens at half-time when the score was 2–1 and forgot to take it off at the re-start of the second half so Celtic's other five goals and the cavalry charge of white horses into the riotous Rangers end could not be shown. Try telling that to a Celtic supporter.
Archie MacPherson, *Action Replays*, 1991.

Gosh, Willie, you might have left that one out.
Reputed remark by Rangers keeper **George Niven** to Celtic's Willie Fernie, after Fernie scored from the last-minute penalty which made it 7–1 to Celtic in the 1957 League Cup final.

'How many people were at the match?' I was asked.
　'Eighty thousand or thereabouts,' I replied.
　'Sixty-six dead out of eighty thousand isn't all that many really!' came the retort.
　To this day I have preferred to allow that remark to be shrouded in anonymity for I do think we owed it to each other to admit afterwards that we had become, by different routes,

emotionally unstable . . . The Old Firm game of January 1971 has, to this day, never been seen on television.
Archie MacPherson recalling the 1971 Ibrox disaster, *Action Replays*, 1991.

I remember one Old Firm tussle when Tommy Gemmell was giving him [Willie Henderson] a hard time. After one foul the wee man crashed to the ground but was up in a flash, waving a finger in Tam's face. The fans were at fever pitch. They expected a barney but of course didn't realise what Willie was saying. As they faced each other only inches apart Willie quipped: 'Any more of that, big man, and we're not going for a pint after the game!'
Jimmy Johnstone, *Jinky – Now and Then*.

In one of my early Old Firm games – the 1978 League Cup semi-final – I was sent off. I was a young lad trying to endear myself to our fans and prove I was one of them. I thought the way to go about it was to run about daft and shout and bawl at the ref. I didn't have the experience to realise I could cause more trouble by playing my own game.
Tommy Burns, March 1991.

They're always tense affairs. I can remember a game at Park-head when John Greig, who was then manager but who'd played in dozens of Old Firm games, came into the dressing-room literally shaking with nerves.
Former Rangers skipper **Ally Dawson**, March 1991.

The best way to sum up those games [local derbies in Italy and France] was that not much football was played. Glasgow derbies are faster and more demanding but more chances are created.
Mark Hateley, March 1991.

I've been involved in Manchester derby games but City–United is like a March wind. The Old Firm's a January hurricane.
Billy McNeill on Old Firm matches, October 1993.

I took my two boys to a Celtic v Rangers match and they'd never seen anything like it in their life. They couldn't believe that when a goal was scored one end of the park would go demented, dancing and singing, while the other end of the

park was absolutely, utterly silent. That sense of excitement is very important in football.
Sean Connery, 1985.

I'm pleased with the two points but it was just a Premier League game, same as any other.
Graeme Souness after the 1–0 win over Celtic, 31 August 1986.

The longer I'm with Rangers the more I realise how important the games with Celtic are. It's more than just two points.
Souness, after the 5–1 win over Celtic, 25 August 1988.

It was as awful an experience as I have ever had against Rangers. In the second half I just prayed and prayed that they wouldn't get to seven.
Celtic's **Tommy Burns** on the same match.

About 3.15 p.m. as I was patrolling near the west end of the stadium, my attention was attracted to an incident near the Rangers goalmouth. I saw that the Rangers goalkeeper Christopher Woods had come out of his goal and had been challenged by the Celtic player Francis McAvennie. I saw McAvennie quite deliberately strike the Rangers keeper Woods with what I would describe as a slap on the face. The Rangers keeper in turn seemed to put his right forearm against McAvennie's face and push him away. The next thing was the Rangers centre-half Butcher joined the other two and they then began to jostle each other. I was then aware of the Rangers football player Graham Roberts running across from the opposite side of the park and I then saw him quite deliberately punch the Celtic player McAvennie on the side of the head, causing McAvennie to fall to the ground. The whole attitude of the crowd was very volatile and it seemed to me that we were in great danger of a pitch invasion.
Inspector James Moir, Strathclyde Police report on the Old Firm match of 17 October 1987.

Rangers have spent £12 million and created a very good stadium. Not one that I personally want for Celtic, but, nevertheless, one which is impressive.
New Celtic chairman **Jack McGinn**, September 1986.

Rangers were in a deep pit and they had to lay out £2.5 million to try to keep up with us.
Celtic director **Tom Grant**, January 1987.

Rangers are becoming totally dependent on the success of their team. They can't develop Ibrox and there's nothing they can build around it. I've never thought Ibrox was a particularly good stadium. It is better than anything else, but I don't think it's a good stadium.
Celtic chief executive **Terry Cassidy** does his bit for Glasgow cultural relations, January 1992.

Those players might as well face facts. They aren't Rangers men through and through. And the Ibrox supporters know it. You can't fool the guys who pay their money every week. They know the ones who play for the jersey and the ones who don't.
Tommy Burns, after watching a stormy Old Firm game, March 1991.

I was called an 'Orange bastard' when I played with Mother-well. With most players it's just a joke, it doesn't bother them.
Brian McClair, February 1987.

The team were magnificent. That's the way football should be played – apart from us not putting the ball in the net. We dominated from start to finish and when you play as well as we did you've got to be happy.
Liam Brady after his side's 1–0 defeat at Ibrox, January 1993. It left Celtic ten points behind leaders Rangers.

One of the most important ones, when I started to think the team had resilience for when things went against them, was when we played Celtic in the semi-final of the Scottish Cup and had David Robertson ordered off in the opening minutes of the match and we had to play virtually the whole of the game with ten men. Celtic came at us as you would expect them to do and that night we showed a spirit that has been evident on more than one occasion. That was the first time I'd realised the squad of players we had were developing a togetherness, if you like, in their approach to the game.
Walter Smith, 1993.

It will be blood and guts, as usual. There is no experience in the world like an Old Firm derby. It takes over your whole mind, and you don't have the time to think. Basically, you just run about like an idiot for 90 minutes.
Charlie Nicholas, October 1993.

I only know the first two lines of *The Sash* because after that we've usually scored.
Roy Aitken on Old Firm rivalry, 1980s.

There will now be a minute's silence . . . as a mark of respect to Rangers, who went out of the European Cup tonight.
Radio Clyde DJ **'Tiger' Tim Stevens'** half-time announcement to the Parkhead crowd during the Celtic v Young Boys Berne UEFA Cup tie, 30 September 1993. Stevens was promptly sacked from his role as Parkhead match MC.

Due to the intransigent attitude of Celtic Football Club and their lack of responsibility with regard to their supporters' behaviour, we believe that no other course of action is now available to us.
Rangers chairman **David Murray**, announcing on 26 January 1994 that they would withhold Celtic's ticket allocation for the season's final Old Firm match after £20,000 worth of damage had been caused to the Ibrox away end since March 1992.

The best lads are people like Peter Grant of Celtic. He's a smashing fellow. He's as Celtic as our boys are Rangers, and you have a respect for that.
Ally McCoist, February 1994.

You very seldom get a particularly good game.
Celtic full-back **Jim Craig** on Old Firm games, *Only a Game?*, BBC documentary, 1985.

Glasgow, where life is taken almost as seriously as football itself.
Only an Excuse '93 stage show.

GOD ON THEIR SIDE (RELIGION)

They [Celtic] sign Protestants because they have no real choice – and then make a virtue of it.
Jim Baxter, *The Party's Over*.

The continued insistence of the Catholic Church in Scotland that Catholic children must remain segregated from Protestants at school can't be a great help to mutual understanding.
William McIlvanney, *Only a Game?*, BBC documentary, 1985.

That there is a club who say . . . not only have you got to be able to play football but you've got to have gone to the right school, I find it incredible in this day and age, apart from anything else. I find it pathetic. I hope, as people have done for 50 years, it'll stop. But I'll believe it when I see it.
Journalist **Ian Archer**, *Only a Game?*, BBC documentary, 1985.

At the root of it all is the separate schools. Those who advocate separate schools are the guilty people, not Rangers Football Club.
Rangers chief executive **Alan Montgomery**, August 1989.

To suggest that the existence of Christian Catholic schools contributes to bigotry demonstrates a breathtaking misunderstanding of Christian teaching as expressed in Catholic schools.
Father Noel Barry, editor of *Flourish*, the official publication of the Archdiocese of Glasgow, responds to Montgomery, August 1989.

There was a woman there with the blue eye-shadow and the red lipstick and I was walking off and she called me a big dirty Fenian bastard. I turned round and said, 'Oh come on,' and she said, 'Nothing personal, I know your Auntie Annie.'
Hibs striker **Tony Higgins** on playing Rangers, *Only a Game?*, BBC documentary, 1985.

They are not lepers. I know, I married one. How could I carry out a policy where I won't sign a Catholic but I'll go home and live with one?
Graeme Souness, September 1986.

I had to laugh. Maurice [Johnston] may have his own privately-held religious beliefs but in any word-association test 'faith' is not what you would automatically put after his name.

Tommy Burns on Maurice Johnston, crossing himself after being sent off in the 1986 League Cup final against Rangers.

Basically, I have to believe the Celtic board rejected the idea of Danny McGrain becoming assistant manager . . . It has been suggested to me that there is another possible explanation. That is the question of me not being a Roman Catholic. I would fervently hope that is very far from the case, given that the best manager the club has ever had was a Protestant.

Danny McGrain, *In Sunshine or in Shadow*, 1987.

The arrival of Rangers in the troubled takeover battle for Scotland striker Maurice Johnston obviously caught the BBC's London-based Ceefax staff on the hop. Their first statement flashed up on screens at breakfast time, described Mo as the first Catholic to sign for Celtic – a normally all-Protestant club. Ceefax is now well aware it has a lot of readers north of the border.

Scotsman Diary, July 1989.

I don't consider it a serious question now. We're past that. If somebody wants to make an issue of it, they're living in the past and they're the bigots, not the modern-day management who are at Rangers today.

David Murray on religion, 1993.

He was a fanatic as he could not see past the Light Blues. If they lost he was deeply affected. But I never once saw my grandad wear a blue scarf or a rosette, and I was certainly not brought up in a background of religious bigotry.

Walter Smith, September 1991.

We're arguably the biggest institution outwith the Church in Scotland.

Rangers chairman **David Murray**, November 1993.

MoJo

A lively bugger, isn't he?
Jock Stein, after Johnston had scored two goals against Spain, November 1984.

It was something which happened while Johnston was with another team. It wouldn't happen while he was with Celtic.
Celtic manager **David Hay** in 1985 after MoJo was fined £200 for reset.

I'm taking the rap for entertaining girls at an early-morning party in the team's hotel the day after we arrived in Australia for last December's qualifying game. The festivities were going full swing then there was a knock at the bedroom door. Alex Ferguson's number two, Walter Smith, was standing outside with an icy look in his eyes. He gave me a curt command: 'Get these girls out of the hotel!' . . . I wasn't alone but I'm the only one to be given the cold shoulder . . . I know I was wrong. But there was only laughs, a few drinks, and anything but an orgy going on . . . If I had been caught alone with a bird, I might have been worried, but this was just a fun party.
Maurice Johnston on why he was left out of the 1986 World Cup squad, May 1986.

Equally serious is the suggestion that I've been left out in the cold because the SFA don't want to risk another drugs scandal . . . going by some of those scurrilous slanders, I'm supposed to be a junkie. And as the boffins have come up with some new dope test that can trace drugs going back six months in the system, I'm always supposed to be too much of a gamble. Believe it or not, I've never taken drugs in my life. Drink, which I can't handle, and women, which I can, are my weakness. I had my house raided by the Drugs Squad last year . . . After turning me over, an officer told me almost apologetically, 'We were acting on a tip-off.'
Maurice Johnston, May 1986.

I might even agree to become Rangers' first Catholic if they paid me £1 million cash and bought me Stirling Castle. Let me spell out where I stand. I am a Celtic man through and through and so I dislike Rangers because they are a force in Scottish football and therefore a threat to the club I love. But more than that I hate the religious policy they maintain. Why won't they sign a Roman Catholic?

Maurice Johnston, in *Mo: An Autobiography*, 1988.

I'll finish my career here. I don't want to play for any other club.

Johnston on agreeing to rejoin Celtic from Nantes, 1989.

It's a dream. I never thought they'd want me back. I had offers from England and the Continent but I wanted to wear the green and white again. Deep down I've always wanted to be back with Celtic.

Johnston, being paraded in a Celtic jersey, 1989.

It's a complete fabrication. You can run that story for ten years and it still wouldn't be true.

Bill McMurdo, Johnston's agent, on stories Rangers wanted to sign him (days before they did), 1989.

There we were, the four of us, sitting in this tiny French café near Orly Airport with a little old Frenchwoman serving us coffee at around ten o'clock in the morning. She must have wondered what on earth we were up to.

Graeme Souness on the venue for the negotiations to sign Johnston on 7 July 1989, *A Manager's Diary*, 1989.

I'm happy to be joining one of the biggest clubs in Europe.

Johnston on signing for Rangers, 10 July 1989.

We have signed Maurice Johnston for Rangers Football Club because he is the best striker in British football at the moment.

Graeme Souness, 1989.

When Johnston's transfer was announced, every other news story paled into insignificance. Genocide in China, the bicentennial of the French Revolution, crisis in the food industry, a national rail strike, cabinet disagreement about the European monetary system – who cares. Rangers had signed a pape.

Stuart Cosgrove, *Hampden Babylon: Sex and Scandal in Scottish Football*, 1991.

Mo joined us in Italy at Il Ciocco and all the English players especially welcomed him and made him feel at home. He had to room with Ally McCoist but I think he roomed with him anyway for Scotland games. The kit man, Jimmy Bell, wouldn't lay out Mo's kit for training in the morning – Mo had to go downstairs and pick that up. He wouldn't lay out his chocolate bars – Ally used to get a chocolate bar of his own when he came round with the rations at night. Mo wasn't accepted at all by the Scottish players and it took a long time in a way for them to accept him.
Terry Butcher recalling his first impressions after the signing, 1993.

Collaborators Can't Play Without Kneecaps.
Graffiti at Glasgow's Bellgrove railway station (near Parkhead), July 1991.

I couldn't believe my ears when people told me Mo should be put down. Others have told me the dog's likely to have its legs broken. What kind of mentality do people have?
Nan O'Malley, Dumbarton dog-owner, after her five-year-old mongrel, Mo, had received death threats as feelings ran high, July 1991.

I remember meeting in my house about three weeks before the deal was announced, sitting in my living-room with Walter Smith, Alan Montgomery, Bill McMurdo, myself and Maurice Johnston, and I'll never forget the golfer who looked over the first fairway at Murrayfield Golf Course, looked into my lounge and I'm sure he rubbed his eyes and said, 'Cannae be!'
David Murray, 1993.

We had to break this tradition that was starting to haunt the club. We're trying to build a football club that's attractive not only to people in Scotland but throughout the world, and carrying on this religious bigotry was not in the best long-term interests\of Rangers Football Club.
David Murray, 1993.

116 Years of Tradition Ended.
Message attached to a wreath delivered to Ibrox by hardline fans, 1989.

The world of Scottish football was rocked to its pre-cast concrete foundations over the close season when Rangers finally broke with 100 years of tradition and bought a player from FC Nantes for the first time in their history.
The Absolute Game fanzine, 1989.

Now that a few years have gone by, it's easy to forget just how volatile a situation he [Johnston] had got himself into. I remember when Mo signed, Graeme Souness asked me to do a TV interview, welcoming the new signing to the club and saying he had all our backing. Terry Butcher had already done one, but the manager wanted a West of Scotland player, like myself or Ian Durrant, to do a similar piece. I refused, not because I wasn't supporting the wee man, the facts were anything but. I told the manager that I would tell Mo to his face he had my 100 per cent backing, and I'd say the same in front of the rest of the team . . . but I was a bit wary of going up-front like that on TV or in the press. I had heard feelings were running high back home, and I didn't want some nutter throwing a brick through my mother's window because he thought I had said the wrong thing.
Ally McCoist, *My Story*, 1992.

When Alastair was the player Graeme decided to axe, the trouble really erupted . . . I'm absolutely convinced that if Mo had been dropped then there would have been little or no fuss. But Graeme was never a man to take the easy way out. He thought that Mo and myself would make the best partnership and that was the end of it as far as he was concerned. He was not about to change his mind because several thousand fans in the enclosure had decided he was wrong.
Mark Hateley, *Top Mark!*

Looking back, I am delighted with the way I handled what was a very difficult situation. I had some extremely low moments but I felt I conducted myself with dignity . . . Look around the globe and see all the people with real problems and it is quite absurd to think of the amount of column inches that were devoted to the fact I wasn't getting a game of football. Don't misunderstand me. At the time I thought I was the most wronged man in the world. Now I see it differently and, hand on heart, I feel no bitterness towards Graeme Souness. He's

had a horrendous year at Liverpool and I honestly hope it works out for him there.
Ally McCoist, February 1993.

He has never shown any indication to get in touch and his behaviour is not endearing Maurice to me.
Andy Roxburgh, January 1992, after MoJo had criticised team selection for the San Marino game in November 1991.

I've gone the last mile with him.
Roxburgh on MoJo after leaving him out of the squad for the friendly against Northern Ireland, 1992.

I don't have a bad word to say about the lad and I think that goes for everyone here. Nobody can tell why he chose Rangers. It was probably that little bit of devil in him. It wasn't easy for him but he had the mentality to handle it. Maurice was devil-may-care, but strong-willed at the same time.
Walter Smith, September 1993.

PRESSURE

When did you last see a professional footballer laugh?
Quoted in Bob Crampsey's obituary of **Matt Busby**, *Glasgow Herald*, 21 January 1994.

There was me saying, 'Oh tremendous pressure on me as Rangers manager', and there would be somebody watching that interview at home who had problems, maybe somebody in the family dying in hospital. I could visualise them saying, 'He ought to be in here and see the pressures we're under. That's only a game they're playing.'
Rangers boss **John Greig**, *Only a Game?*, BBC documentary, 1985.

The pressure on match days is making my head explode. I can't go on.
Kenny Dalglish, resigning as Liverpool boss, 1991.

Five grand a week? That's my kind of pressure.
Birmingham boss **Lou Macari** after Dalglish's departure, 1991.

Pressure to me is being homeless or unemployed. This isn't pressure, it's pleasure.
Scotland coach **Andy Roxburgh** after naming 17 players who were unavailable to him for the game against Germany, 1993.

Everyone has pressure, whatever walk of life they are in. I happen to like the aggravation that goes with football management. It seems to suit my needs.
Graeme Souness, the day he was appointed Liverpool manager, 1991.

The pressure of playing for a team like that is indescribable. The last year I played, when we were going for the championship, I wasn't getting to sleep at night.
Alan Hansen on playing for Liverpool, April 1993.

BLACK IS BLACK

One of the great delusions of Scottish society is the widespread belief that Scotland is a tolerant and welcoming country and that racism is a problem confined to England's green unpleasant land.
Stuart Cosgrove, *Hampden Babylon: Sex and Scandal in Scottish Football*, 1991.

[Giles] Heron only stayed at Parkhead a couple of seasons, long enough to become embittered by unfriendly Scottish winters and enchanted by the attention of a local Glasgow girl called Margaret who he met at the dancing. The couple are happily married and live in Detroit, where Giles Heron still enjoys ridiculing his black friends with the word 'darkie', which he relishes saying in a pantomime Scots accent.
Stuart Cosgrove, *Hampden Babylon: Sex and Scandal in Scottish Football*, 1991.

The Scots booed me because of my colour. It started at the warm-up and went on when I scored. I was even spat on. It was the saddest night of my football life.
Dutch striker **Ruud Gullit** recalls playing for Feyenoord in the UEFA Cup against St Mirren, September 1983.

The player was struck by a banana, which is a missile. A missile is a missile in whatever form.
Rangers operations executive **Alastair Hood** after Mark Walters was pelted with fruit during the game against Hearts, January 1988.

The racial abuse I've suffered in Scotland is far worse than anything I had to put up with in England or Italy.
Paul Elliott, soon after signing for Celtic, 1989.

I seemed to experience problems particularly when we were at Hearts and Hibs. The racist abuse was often quite severe, although generally restricted to a minority in the standing areas. Funnily enough, I also remember when we played Hearts at Parkhead their supporters absolutely terrorised me with racist insults – so much so that John Colquhoun, the Hearts player and SPFA representative, made several attempts to express his disapproval of their behaviour . . . Some people suggested that the abuse arose simply because I played for Celtic . . . however, this was possibly their way of 'sweeping the matter under the carpet' instead of accepting it and dealing with it.

Ex-Celt **Paul Elliott**, *The Absolute Game* fanzine, May 1992.

If children see people showing this 18th-century attitude they might think it's acceptable. If they grow up thinking that, the country will be in disarray.

Falkirk's **Richard Cadette** on racist abuse, December 1992.

When we were playing Hamilton last Saturday, a group of six guys were giving me the usual sort of abuse. After about ten minutes it died out apart from one guy who kept shouting that I was a black bastard. About 25 minutes into the game he was still the only one at it and I turned and told him to shut up because no one was listening to him. I didn't hear him after that.

Falkirk striker **Richard Cadette**, at the launch of a SPFA Campaign For Racial Equality initiative, January 1993.

It's the way Cadette plays that attracts attention. Brian Rice took a fair bit of stick because he has reddish hair.

St Mirren's chairman **Allan Marshall**'s response to complaints that Falkirk's Richard Cadette had been booked for reacting to racist taunts, January 1994.

TRAGEDY

I remember little about the visit [to West Ham] except the sign that I saw on my way out: 'Remember Ibrox. Please Leave Slowly.'
Bill Buford, *Among the Thugs*, 1991.

Everything went to plan. The sun blazed down on a glorious April afternoon, we played some beautiful football, and deserved our win. One of the high points of my career came when I scored the only goal of the game to send us to one of the most glamorous occasions in world sport, the FA Cup final. I almost floated off the park, amid the deafening noise of the delirious Evertonians. This would be a day to remember. Unfortunately, it turned out to be one you couldn't forget, even if you wanted to.
Pat Nevin, recalling scoring Everton's winner in the FA Cup semi-final on the day of the Hillsborough disaster, February 1994.

TOUGH GUYS

The Premier League in Scotland is the most physical, cynical and brutal league in the world. You hear people talking about wild tackling in Spain . . . I don't think any of their hatchet-men would be able to live with some of those in our league.

Jim McLean, *Jousting With Giants*, 1987.

If he'd carried on as a manager he'd have ended up in a wooden box. He'd batter his granny to get a result.

Rangers defender **John Brown** on the Ibrox side's assistant manager (and Brown's boss at Dundee), Archie Knox, 1993.

I never thought of taking him off, even with a broken nose. They're nothing. I tried to get one throughout my career because they add character to your face.

George Graham, after the 1993 FA Cup final in which Andy Linighan scored the winner with a broken nose.

WHACK!

I just could not believe my ears.

Rangers defender **Willie Woodburn** after being banned *sine die* by the SFA, 14 September 1954. The 34-year-old had been sent off – for the fourth time in his career – against Stirling Albion two weeks earlier.

I probably took the mickey too much. A frustrated player can strike out in anger. I asked for it.

Jim Baxter after a tackle by Rapid Vienna's Skocik left him with a broken leg, December 1964.

During my time in the game I have been dismissed prematurely about 15 times, a statistic I would prefer to ignore. But it takes an awful lot of ignoring.

Willie Johnston, *On the Wing!*

Very few players go through such a long career as mine without badly fouling, intentionally or unintentionally, another player. Possibly John McMaster will understand that.

Willie Johnston, *On the Wing!* Johnston had been sent off for a brutal foul on McMaster in a League Cup tie against Aberdeen, September 1980. McMaster required the kiss of life on the park.

I am a professional and I had to stop the Scotland player, Nicholas, from scoring. I would do the same again.

Denmark midfielder **Claus Berggren** on his professional foul on Charlie Nicholas, Scotland v Denmark, World Cup, June 1986.

He's kicked people down here and now I suppose he's going to kick them up in Scotland.

David Pleat on Graham Roberts signing for Rangers, 1986.

I met him afterwards in the players lounge and told him to his face he was an absolute nutcase.

Aston Villa skipper **Allan Evans** on Southampton's Mark Dennis, who'd just been sent off for the tenth time, December 1986.

I was nearly a goner. It's only because I head the ball a lot that I'm here to talk about it.

Aston Villa's **Andy Gray** after landing on his head during a friendly, February 1987.

The type of player I have been, maybe it should have happened to me. I have given out a few knocks and I have taken a few knocks myself – so maybe this one I could have taken. I might even have thought it was a balancing up of the books. Who knows, maybe I would have deserved it!

Graeme Souness on Ian Durrant's knee injury, *A Manager's Diary*, 1989.

I'm not concerned with the game of football. What does concern me very much indeed is the prevention of public disorder in connection with sporting events. A large percentage of supporters are readily converted by breaches of the peace on the field into two rival mobs. That they were not so transformed is no credit to you.

Sheriff **Archibald McKay**, April 1988, fining Terry Butcher £250 for breach of the peace at the Old Firm match of October 1987.

FITNESS

It takes a fair bit of strength to move full-grown pigs around.
Queen of the South striker (and pig farmer) **Rowan Alexander** on signing for St Mirren, June 1983.

There's one bit of advice I'd give people. Train. Get fit. It's the easiest thing in the world to get fit if you're young. But I was lazy. Dave Mackay said to me, the time'll come when you want to train and you can't do it, and that came true. The time came when I'd get put out of a game by guys I wouldn't have shit on ten years before. That was why I stopped at 30. I wasn't fit.
Jim Baxter, *Only a Game?*, BBC documentary, 1985.

One day we were playing Rangers at Ibrox. I was taking a corner and couldn't focus on the ball. It felt like I had lead boots on . . . I reckon I missed three years at the top and two in the lower divisions.
Former Celtic and Scotland winger **Davie Provan**, February 1993, forced to quit football through ME in 1986.

Stamina: I should give him 12 out of 10, but I'm not really an expert on the subject.
Jim Baxter on the Celtic captain, Paul McStay, 1992.

Right now, definitely. Ask me in five years and it might be different.
Jim Duffy, on whether playing again was worth constant knee pain, October 1992. Duffy returned to play two and a half years after a 1987 knee injury forced him to quit football.

When I started playing again three years ago, the only insurance policy I could get said, 'Exclusions: Right leg'.
Dundee player-boss **Jim Duffy**, October 1993.

Now I know that as soon as a coach starts talking about fitness

he is useless, he hasn't got a clue. For goodness sake, you can't play football if you're not fit to run 90 minutes, it's bloody logical. This game is all about skill.
Dundee United boss **Ivan Golac**, February 1994.

THE GAME

There are Prime Ministers and Sports Ministers and other Ministers who are trying to tell us how to administer football. They known nothing at all about the game of football. They're trying to run football and most of them have never been to a football game.
Jock Stein, *Only a Game?*, BBC documentary, 1985.

J. B. Priestley said football was both hurtling with conflict, and yet passionate and beautiful in its art. Now to me that's Scottish football. It was a remarkable statement, especially as the guy was English.
Andy Roxburgh, then SFA director of coaching, *Only a Game?*, BBC documentary, 1985.

Soccer's a volatile game. It's not Chinese chequers.
Dundee's Canadian chairman, **Ron Dixon**, June 1993.

Football in Scottish life is about much more than sport. It's really the arena in which Scotland and Scots assert themselves and play a role in international affairs.
Dr Henry Drucker, Edinburgh University, *Only a Game?*, BBC documentary, 1985.

To actually see the live theatre, 22,000 customers there, the players enjoying themselves, and the whole vibrance of that – that in itself is reward.
Hearts chairman **Wallace Mercer**, *Only a Game?*, BBC documentary, 1985.

Football takes itself too seriously. Chairmen take themselves too seriously. Football is about heroes and villains. There's a lot more serious things in life. In fact, football really should be about escapism.
Hearts chairman **Wallace Mercer**, *Only a Game?*, BBC documentary, 1985.

The amount of time-wasting and attempts to deceive referees by players feigning injury or diving to get fellow professionals into trouble has all contributed towards making the game far

less enjoyable than it was before. We have all lost our conscience and can't even see how low we have stooped.
Jim McLean, February 1989.

The game has blossomed into this unhealthy obsession with
blinkered national arrogance and the clinging to fanaticism and
mindless tribal bigotries that we all know and love.
It's Only an Excuse, BBC Radio spoof documentary, 1986.

And on the sixth day, God was bored out of his skull,
And he spake unto what he had created thus far, saying:
Where there be harmony,
Let there be discord.
Where there be unity,
Let there be divisions.
Where there be tolerance,
Let there be suspicion.
Where there be Proddy,
Let there be Tim.
Where there be bigotry,
Let there be bampotry.
Where there are balloons,
Let there be broadcasters.
Where there is truth,
Let there be exclusives.
Where there are phones,
Let there be phone-ins.
Where there is a nation,
Let there be late injury call-offs.
Where there was sanity,
Let there be football.
Only an Excuse '93 stage show.

Scottish football – once a simple game played by semi-illiter-
ates. Now a multi-million-pound industry played by semi-
illiterates.
Only an Excuse '93 stage show.

It was 100-miles-an-hour stuff and I remember thinking afterwards, 'God almighty, is it going to be like this every week?'
Martin Hayes on his Celtic debut at Motherwell, August 1990. He was
substituted, Celtic finished with ten men and lost 2-0.

If I was 18 again, I certainly wouldn't stay here. Strength has replaced skill as the most important credential for playing. When you watch teams on the Continent in action, every player seems comfortable on the ball. With the exception of Rangers and Celtic, there are only two or three players in most Premier League sides who can say the same thing. The standard now is a lot worse than it was when I began playing in the Premier League 14 seasons ago. It's reached the stage now where if you can put your foot on the ball and slow the game down you stick out a mile.
Davie Cooper, March 1991.

There is little doubt Scottish football is worse off now than it was five years ago, and someone will have to find a way to convince everyone else that self-interest is not healthy for the game.
Walter Smith after all five Scots clubs had gone out of Europe in the opening two rounds, November 1993.

There will be plenty of people who disagree with me, but I honestly believe that footballers must have the very best of facilities.
Gordon Strachan, *Strachan Style*, 1991.

I don't know if I'll miss football once I'm finished.
Paul McStay, February 1987.

Football is always going to be conservative by its nature. It's run by old men. In anything, not just football, older people don't want to change things. They're scared.
Brian McClair, February 1987.

Football is a very conservative game and people in it are frightened of anyone who speaks his mind. I'm always amazed at the attitude some men in Scottish football have towards the Professional Footballers' Association. It's obviously regarded as a sinister body by some, instead of one seeking to get the best for its members. The peculiar thing is that many respect secretary Tony Higgins, while I get vibes that they're wary of me.
Scottish Professional Footballers' Association chairman **Fraser Wishart**, November 1992.

Football was never a family game. Quite honestly, there's nothing worse at a match than half a dozen kids running around your feet who are not interested.

Gwen McIlroy, author of Dundee United book, *A View from the Ground*, August 1993.

[Football is] one of the great things in this world. I remember they ran a competition to write a football song on *Nationwide*. The one that won it, called 'Where Are You Now, Joe Ackroyd?' was gorgeous – an old guy talking about what football had meant to him, in its biggest sense. I never found out who wrote it, but I remember thinking, good on you, football deserves that. People love it, and it is important.

Dundonian songwriter **Michael Marra**.

In my 17 years at Ibrox I never once got out of bed and thought, 'Oh Christ, I've got to go there today'. I loved it; couldn't get there early enough. I was at the ground for training at 9.10 in the morning and we didn't start until 10.15. I played head tennis for an hour before we started. I played it again after we finished. You see, those were the greatest days of my life.

Hibs boss **Alex Miller**, February 1994.

Football . . . it's basic. It's like opening yourself up to a psychoanalyst. I can tell people's characters by the way they play football – the way they react to a foul against them, or to the referee or when they score a goal. You can't tell everything, but you can tell a lot.

Graeme Souness, November 1990.

I don't subscribe to the theory that we play too much football here. I'd play every night of the week given the chance.

Celtic boss **Lou Macari**, November 1993.

Getting to the last European Championship finals hid a multitude of sins. As usual we had been handicapping ourselves because of the number of games we play and the way we play them. However, when it came to the World Cup qualifiers the bubble burst.

Andy Roxburgh, December 1993.

To the Scots, football's a lovely incurable disease.

Tommy Docherty, *Only a Game?*, BBC documentary, 1985.

HOW IT'S DONE

Keep playing to the fat man.
Brian Clough team talks at Nottingham Forest, 1980s. The fat man was John Robertson.

You can make a player fitter by giving him a pay rise. It might sound daft, but he works harder and he's happier at home.
Swindon boss **Lou Macari**, 1988.

I never went for aerial challenges at Liverpool. You lose 150 brain cells every time you head a ball. I used to make Mark Lawrenson do all the heading. You have to delegate. It's a captain's prerogative.
Alan Hansen, April 1993.

HAMPDEN

The only ground that looks the same in black and white as it does in colour.
David Lacey, *The Guardian*, 1987.

That it [Hampden] was named after an English patriot might have been judged anathema to most Scots.
Russell Galbraith, *The Hampden Story*, 1993. Hampden was named after Hampden Terrace overlooking the ground, itself named in honour of politician John Hampden, killed in the English Civil War in 1643.

It is the most magnificent stadium I have ever seen, the life and essence of football.
Hungary's **Ferenc Puskas** on Hampden, December 1954.

We missed playing our home games at Hampden.
Andy Roxburgh after Scotland failed to qualify for the 1994 World Cup, April 1993.

Nobody needs to buy a new pair of shoes after a trip to Hampden now. I suspect the only people who will not be pleased with the work that's been done are the shoe salesmen and the cobblers.
Jim Farry after Hampden's £12 million redevelopment, November 1993.

The reason why we all go back, despite the rain, despite the urine, despite the macaroon bars, despite the turgid football, despite the Pandas, despite the awful conditions, is that every so often something happens which makes it all worthwhile. Like England scoring two own goals, as in 1974. Or Charlie Nicholas uncorking a beauty, as against Switzerland in 1983. Or Donachie's supernatural own-goal against Wales. Or the entire Uruguayan team leaving the field and refusing to play on after an offside decision went against them in '83, Clemence letting the ball through his legs, Gordon McQueen colliding with a goal-post, Jim Holton colliding with everything else, Dalglish's goal against Spain, Derek Johnstone's 30-yard header against Wales, grown men from Paisley weeping with joy after the Cup final in '87, grown men from Dundee weeping after every Cup final . . . We're Scottish! We like a bit of suffering with our pleasure! Whether Hampden is converted into a people's palace or left to rot as a gigantic folly, I somehow doubt if its unique ability to lift you out of the mundane into the realms of real cerebral ecstasy can be recaptured in any other context . . . You either got soul or you don't. Hampden had it.

Alastair McSporran, *The Absolute Game* fanzine, October 1992.

SCOTLAND

The Scots as a nation passionately believe that they should be the best at everything and are disappointed when they are not.
Graeme Souness, *No Half Measures*, 1985.

The Scotland team is more than just a football team. It's a symbol of everything we would like to be as a nation – flamboyant, exciting, glamorous and colourful. The reality is that we have a pretty grey world up here in Scotland but for 90 minutes we can forget all that at Hampden on a big night.
Andy Roxburgh, November 1986.

In his playing days, Ally MacLeod was a winger of the first order, and he made it clear that as a manager he saw that breed as an integral and essential part of a successful team. That was the best news I had heard since I was told I could leave school. If MacLeod wanted a winger, then he would get one with bells on!
Willie Johnston, *On the Wing!*

There are times when I think he [Andy Roxburgh] overdoes it and could be said to pamper the players. The idea of taking the Scotland team to the opulent splendour of the Gleneagles Hotel in Perthshire, for instance, is a move of dubious merit. And I do not say that as a veteran survivor of the bad old days in the Queen's Hotel, Largs, where a squad of players would race each other back from training because there were only three baths in the whole place and the internal plumbing system was so eccentric that all three could not be run at the same time. That was one neglectful extreme, but taking players to this repository for the well-to-do is surely the other end of the spectrum. If the living is too easy can there be any burning desire to play a hard game of football? I would imagine that going out and, in the grand old cliché, dying for the jersey would be the last thing on your mind.
Danny McGrain, *In Sunshine or in Shadow*, 1987.

The international team depends on the goodwill of member clubs. If we are to qualify for the World Cup it is imperative we receive the wholehearted support of everyone concerned.
International Committee Chairman **Ian Gellatly**, announcing the SFA would meet Rangers in a bid to offset the Ibrox side's reluctance to release players for Scotland, January 1988.

Maybe it's the wrong thing to say but I honestly don't feel I'm up to international football. I believe that you have to set standards and I wouldn't like to come and watch an international team with Jim McInally in it. I'd rather watch a Scotland team full of Paul McStays, players with exceptional ability.
Dundee United's **Jim McInally**, 1988.

Scotland are in the World Cup finals and the guy who's in charge wears a wig and has a nose that could cut a wedding cake.
Craig Brown on Andy Roxburgh, 1990.

People keep portraying me as a pragmatist and a tactician. I'm not. I'm a supporter, a Scotland fan. If Craig and I weren't in charge of the team we'd be on the terracing. I'm a victim of my own emotions, just like anyone else. When we scored the winner against Cyprus, we were dancing round the track. It's not the way I like to behave but it was an emotional moment.
Andy Roxburgh, 1990.

Roxburgh's a ned. Good on preparation, crap on football.
Terry Butcher quoted in *All Played Out* by Pete Davies, 1990.

I found it difficult scoring goals for Partick Thistle. That's something I always keep in mind when telling Mo Johnston how it's done.
Andy Roxburgh, 1990.

People are always saying what a great team we had back in the 1950s and 1960s . . . We might have beaten England at Wembley occasionally, but so what? The world at large didn't care, however enjoyable it might have been for us.
Andy Roxburgh, July 1991.

When I got to Glasgow Airport I saw it in print – headlines blaring to the whole country that I had been fit but had not played . . . After these trips Andy has a set routine where he goes round all the players to shake their hands – such a lovely guy, you know – and there he is coming towards me with his hand outstretched . . . How could the man want to shake my hand after the stories he had told? I knocked his hand away, just slapped it aside . . . To be honest, I came very close to hitting him.

Richard Gough on the European Championship game against Switzerland, September 1991, *Field of Dreams*.

I was never good enough to play for Scotland and I would never, repeat never, deprive any Rangers player of such an honour. We told the Scottish management that Richard was injured before he left for Switzerland. I will not condone any suggestion that the player pulled out for any other reason.

Walter Smith, September 1991.

This was vintage Scotland. Defending that would bring shame and disgrace on a Sunday League pub team. Atrocious finishing. A heart-stopping, edge-of-your-seats, spray-the-living-room-ceiling-with-the-contents-of-the-nearest-beer-can comeback. The Tartan Army going mental. And to nicely round it off we even had a good old-fashioned after-match controversy.

The Absolute Game fanzine on Scotland's draw in Switzerland, October 1991.

By the time Andy had been in charge for a couple of internationals he had probably called more meetings than Big Jock and Fergie put together . . . It reached the stage where Andy seemed to be calling meetings to arrange still more meetings.

Richard Gough, *Field of Dreams*.

I was wearing my tracksuit bottoms when Craig Brown told me to take them off. 'All the players have to look the same,' he told me. I pointed out how cold it was and kept them on. I don't think he ever forgave me.

Richard Gough discussing a training session before the Scotland game in Belgium, 1987, *Field of Dreams*.

I have always tried to be an honest person. Maybe some day people will think that at least I was saying what I felt was right. Maybe if a lot of other people put their hands on their hearts they would like to have said them as well. The thing about football in this country is that people don't stand up and say what they think. They're too afraid of what might happen to them.
Richard Gough, January 1994.

I left school to get away from teachers bossing me around. Andy Roxburgh is just a headmaster.
Frank McAvennie, January 1992.

The ball hit a water sprinkler and shot high into the air. It was purely an instinctive reaction when he grabbed the ball as it flew over his head.
Andy Roxburgh on the incident leading to Richard Gough's ordering-off against Switzerland, 1992.

Graeme Souness simply laughed each time Andy Roxburgh's name was mentioned.
Richard Gough, *Field of Dreams.*

It's like seeing Scotland score a goal. You never get used to it.
Rod Stewart on the birth of his daughter, 1991.

A great enthusiast. Put him in a junior match and he'd approach it with the same vigour as he would an international.
Motherwell boss **Tommy McLean** on Scotland skipper Gary McAllister, October 1993.

Listening to what seven hundred people at Shawfield could say when things were going badly inoculated me. Seventy thousand couldn't upset me.
Craig Brown, 1989.

A good team with strong English character.
Ruud Gullit before the European Championship match in Sweden, 1992.

Big Roy [Aitken] was unbelievable before the game, noising up the Swedes. He told Mo Johnston to spit at Glenn Hysen's feet

in the tunnel. Mo said, 'He'll probably trap it and play it up the park.'
Andy Goram on Aitken's motivational powers.

I still think I'm the best man for the Scotland job at the moment, but the competition is hotting up. Eoin Jess and Duncan Ferguson are round the corner waiting to take over and that'll happen soon. When it does, good luck to them. I'll go quietly, dig out my tartan scarf and join my mates in the stand.
Ally McCoist, February 1993.

I didn't read any sane, commonsense article saying, well, that's the end of the run lads, it was a wonderful run, and great fun while it lasted, thank you football! A country of five million, to be at five consecutive World Cups, the rest of the world are goggle-eyed at what we achieved. But all you hear from the newspapers is what a load of rubbish, sack the lot, they've let us down, they're a disgrace. It's absurd.
Former SFA secretary **Ernie Walker**, after Scotland had lost 5-0 to Portugal in Lisbon, April 1993.

I don't think there is any working relationship possible between the manager and myself.
Richard Gough announcing he won't play for Scotland under Andy Roxburgh, May 1993.

I feel what he has said and the timing of his announcement embarrasses only him. As the manager who gave him the privilege of captaining Scotland and entering the Hall of Fame I don't think I should add to his embarrassment by saying anything else.
Andy Roxburgh responds, June 1993.

Eighteen years of urban guerilla warfare.
Andy Roxburgh on his years with the SFA, December 1993.

Don't forget his [Andy Roxburgh's] European record: first Scotland manager ever to be caught shagging.
Only an Excuse '93 stage show.

ABERDEEN

Though Aberdeen as it is now known did not come into existence until 1903, the district was made somewhat famous by the efforts of two clubs – Victoria United and Orion. The latter had in it a strong leaven of the scholastic profession, and at one time no fewer than four headmasters were players.
The Football Encyclopædia, 1934.

I was screaming like a banshee all night and ripping the plaster off. My foot was going blue because they'd put it on too tight.
Aberdeen's **Willie Garner** on Bulgarian health care after breaking his leg against Marek Stanke Dimitrov, September 1978.

Drew Jarvie piped up, 'Come on lads, three quick goals and we're back in it.' There was a stunned silence for a minute or two until we grasped the full meaning of his words. Three quick goals against a Liverpool team undefeated at Anfield for almost two years! It was priceless.
Alex Ferguson on being 3–0 behind on aggregate at half-time in the 1980–81 European Cup tie against Liverpool, A Light in the North, 1985.

I remember going with Aberdeen to meet them [Liverpool] at Anfield. We were like boys against men.
Reading boss **Mark McGhee**, January 1994.

For my money he was, at one stage in his career, the best penalty-box defender in the world.
Gordon Strachan on Willie Miller, Strachan Style, 1991.

I think, having all played professionally, we know a bit about the game.
Aberdeen vice-chairman **Chris Anderson** on the club's three-man board, Only a Game? BBC documentary, 1985.

Pittodrie is the hardest place to go in Scottish football. It's like a British boxer going to Italy. You have to knock them out to get a draw.
Hamilton boss **John Lambie**, August 1986.

He [Billy Bingham] asked me if I was interested in playing in Northern Ireland's next under-21 fixture and gave me a week to decide. Although my dad was born in Northern Ireland and we still have a big family in Belfast there was never really going to be any dilemma about which country I would turn out for. Playing for Scotland was one of my dreams as a kid.
Aberdeen's **Eoin Jess**, February 1993.

If I'd a tenner for every stitch I've had over the years I'd have a bank book like Marco Van Basten's.
Aberdeen's battle-scarred defender **Alex McLeish**, October 1993.

It's a fallacy to think that good players can't play on that kind of surface, that you have to bring in the big guns. If anything, the opposite is true. The likes of Connor, Grant, Mason and Nicholas get that extra second to think about things, and they can wrong-foot defenders more easily.
Alex Smith after Aberdeen won 6-2 on a heavy Firhill pitch, January 1990.

Like shooting wee ducks at a fairground to try and win a prize.
Aberdeen manager **Alex Smith** after his side's Scottish Cup final win over Celtic on penalties, 1990.

We are like the old-time miners when the annual Fair Holiday fortnight came round. They would get their wages on Friday morning, but still have a shift to do before they could go on holiday. Our position is the same.
Aberdeen boss **Alex Smith** before the Championship decider at Ibrox, 1991. Needing a draw, Aberdeen lost 2–0 and Rangers won the league.

I thought football looked a cushy life compared to four years at university. I was right!
Aberdeen's **Gary Smith**, who has eight 'O' levels and six Highers, March 1992.

I suggested it was probably best not to try to play offside in his own six-yard box, which was another strange habit he'd picked up.
Former Falkirk boss **Jim Duffy** recalling Gary Smith as a youngster, March 1992.

There was always a bit of a fear that you'd bump into the wrong people . . . I made sure my badge was well covered all the way to the stadium.

Eoin Jess recalling his days as a Rangers 'S' form, March 1993.

I'm a complete waste of time outside the penalty area.

Duncan Shearer, March 1993.

It was always my ambition to win the Camanachd Cup at shinty . . . My dad is still a shinty man through and through. He's never even seen me play football. I know for a fact that on a Saturday night he still looks for the shinty results first, then for how Aberdeen have got on.

Duncan Shearer, March 1993.

At Aberdeen the punters accepted where my heart lay. When I scored against Celtic, I never celebrated, or showed any emotion.

Charlie Nicholas, October 1993.

AIRDRIE

The first penalty kick act took place on the Airdrieonians ground three days after adoption by the Scottish Association on Saturday, 6 January 1891.
The Football Encyclopædia, 1934.

We ended up playing football and that doesn't suit our style.
Alex MacDonald after defeat at Aberdeen, 1991.

We can thank certain sections of the Scottish press for this, because of the unfair stick they have handed out to us over the past year.
Airdrie chairman **George Peat** on UEFA's decision to appoint two trouble-shooters for the European Cup-Winners' Cup tie against Sparta Prague, September 1992, because of concern over Airdrie's rugged style (presumably forgetful of the fact Airdrie were fined £5000 by the SFA two months before for having 14 players sent off and 153 yellow cards the previous season).

Airdire [*sic*] Bank On Big-Match Spur.
Daily Express headline, 12 September 1992.

If he [goalkeeper John Martin] doesn't get at least one daft photo in the *Daily Record* every week he feels he's failing in his duty.
Skipper **Jimmy Sandison**, August 1993.

'Queen of Diamonds'.
Sun headline after bisexual Justin Fashanu's move to Airdrie, 1993.

I wouldn't like to play in the same team as him or even get changed in the vicinity of him.
Wimbledon's **John Fashanu**, on brother Justin's bisexuality, in BBC documentary, *Them and Us*, 1991.

When I die I want my epitaph to read: Here lies Justin Fashanu. He *Lived*!
Justin Fashanu, March 1993.

AIRDRIE

You can't take anything away from Airdrie, apart from maybe their chibs and Doc Martens.
Only an Excuse '93 stage show.

It was a tactical substitution. And make sure you use the word 'tactical' and my name in the same sentence.
Alex MacDonald, February 1994.

We wait for the crowd to fall asleep then we send him on.
Alex MacDonald on sub Andy Smith's interesting role, February 1994.

Nobody wants to lose when their grannies and aunties are watching.
Alex MacDonald psyches his men up for the Scottish Cup tie against Dundee United, March 1994.

ALBION ROVERS

One of the players disagreed so violently with my judgment that we finished the 'discussion' on the waste ground outside Cliftonhill. But he got his jotters just the same.
Albion Rovers chairman **Tom Fagan** on releasing players during his early days on the board, February 1979.

The directors will be running the club and picking the team at the start until Andy settles in.
Albion Rovers chairman **Tom Fagan**, on the appointment of Andy Ritchie as player-coach, June 1984.

Tom Fagan was in charge of picking the team.
Andy Ritchie resigning, August 1984.

He [Joao Havelange, president of FIFA] says, 'Who are you?' I says, 'Albion Rovers.' He says, 'Never heard of them.' I said, 'You ignorant bugger.' But it was a natural thing. I mean, it wisnae him alone – there were other people who'd never heard of Albion Rovers.
Tom Fagan on a meeting of great men, 1985.

[Albion] Rovers were supposed to play Morton in a Reserve League West match on Tuesday night, but referee Jim Hardie decided the game could not be played after he found one of the crossbars to be five inches too low. Perhaps goalies have been swinging on the bar too often but exactly how it came to drop below the legal limit remains a mystery, like many aspects of life in Monklands.
Glasgow Herald, April 1993.

I was driving up a hill and a Capri pulled out in front of me from a junction. I swerved to avoid him just as the works bus came over the hill. I couldn't miss it. The car was a total write-off and I can remember just after the crash I had to hold my jaw up in my hands. The windscreen had shattered and the glass had torn right through my face . . . The guy in the Capri didn't stop and I still don't know who he was. It all puts an 11–1 defeat into perspective.

Albion Rovers keeper **Ronnie McConnachie** after losing 11 goals to Partick Thistle, September 1993.

I was so upset when they scored that I went to kick the ball back into my own net, but I completely missed the goal. I'm the last guy who would want to hit a young girl who was just there to see a game of football.

The unfortunate **Ronnie McConnachie** after hitting a 15-year-old schoolgirl in the face with the ball during a game against Stranraer, February 1994. He was reported to police.

ALLOA ATHLETIC

Not long into the 1987–88 season our Dominic [Sullivan] said goodbye to the manager's job, but at least a contributory factor in him doing so – disillusionment over the team having to use a carpark as a training ground – won marks for originality.

Brian Crosland, *The Absolute Game* fanzine, April 1990.

ARBROATH

On 15 November [1884] Rangers lost a tie at Arbroath but protested that the pitch was two feet short of the minimum fifty yards. 'Beaten on a back green' said the furious telegram sent after the game. The SFA at first decided to let the result stand but, following renewed protests by Rangers, it was compelled to recognise its own rules and ordered a replay which the Glasgow club duly won 8-1. These events would appear to have been traumatic for Arbroath since they were to wait 90 years for their next success against Rangers, a 3-2 win in a league match.

Hugh Keevins and Kevin McCarra, *100 Cups: The Story of the Scottish Cup*, 1985.

The first round saw the by-now expected event of Arbroath wreaking havoc on the hapless Aberdonians. On 3 September 1887 they beat Orion 18–0, the margin of humiliation only being checked by a 'really brilliant goalkeeper'. Perhaps Orion [later to be one of three clubs who merged to form Aberdeen] had him to thank for the improvement on the 1886 Cup tie scoreline of 20–0 to Arbroath. Worse still for the Granite City had been the results on 12 September 1885 when Harp [of Dundee] beat Aberdeen Rovers 35–0 while Arbroath were surpassing even that margin by beating Bon Accord 36–0. Bon Accord had unwisely chosen to waive their right to home advantage. By 17 December 1887 Arbroath's chastisement of their neighbours in numerous Cup ties and friendlies that season had, it was reported, allowed forward Stephen Buick to accumulate 88 goals.

Hugh Keevins and Kevin McCarra, *100 Cups: The Story of the Scottish Cup*, 1985.

The most famous football result in history, Arbroath 36, Bon Accord 0, tells only half the story. The Bon Accord goalkeeper had no time to feel sorry for himself as the following week he won the first of his many international caps for Scotland.

It's Only an Excuse, BBC Radio Scotland spoof documentary, 1986.

If Arbroath sacked me tomorrow I could always get a job on the street selling matches.
Albert Henderson, March 1977. He'd been Arbroath manager for 14 years.

AYR UNITED

I didn't think Ayr could be a Rangers or Celtic, but I did think they could become a Dundee United.

David Murray, on his bid to take over Ayr before he became Rangers chairman, 1990.

BERWICK RANGERS

It is the mark of the beast to leave a trail of havoc and damage.
R. C. Blackhall, chairman of the Berwick Board of Trade, after fans of the
Rangers from Glasgow had caused £1000-worth of damage following a
Scottish Cup tie, January 1960.

It should have been 3–0. We missed easier chances than the
one Sammy Reid scored from.
Berwick player-boss **Jock Wallace** after his side beat Rangers in the Scottish
Cup, 28 January 1967.

Damage? There was no damage. The Glasgow fans couldn't
get away quickly enough.
Berwick police spokesman, January 1967.

Before I went in for the op the surgeon told me I must reconcile
myself to the idea of never playing again. I went in convincecd
football was finished for me. But afterwards he said he'd put
two steel pins in my knee and I'd be all right. They're still
there and I'm still playing.
Sammy Reid, scorer of Berwick's goal, 1967.

The foreman was good enough to give me a bit of extra time
away, so I had to make that up today.
Sammy Reid reporting for work as a gear cutter in a Motherwell engineering
works on Sunday, 29 January 1967, the day after the Rangers match.

They did not play as Rangers players should. The play of some
of them made me sick.
Rangers chairman **John Lawrence**, 30 January 1967.

I do not think we will be able to hold him. He will become one
of the great managers in football.
Berwick chairman **Dr James Sadler** on Jock Wallace after Berwick beat
Rangers, 1967.

Berwick was a great thing for me. The week before the Cup tie
I had the flu and was in my bed. I only got out of my bed on

the Saturday when Berwick beat Rangers. I was still in the reserves and on the Monday I went into Ibrox and there was a complete depression over the place. I was told to pick up my gear and go to the first-team dressing-room. I went along and stripped there and on the Saturday I made my debut against Hearts.

Sandy Jardine on the aftermath of Berwick.

BRECHIN CITY

Their ground, Glebe Park, Brechin, is quite a commodious little enclosure.
The Football Encyclopædia, 1934.

Here in the Glebe Street Hall of Fame, I look up at the roll of honour and read the endless list of famous and revered players who have graced the club: MacLairdie, Bimmie, Tochar, Trialist. In their long and illustrious history, 1906–86 – or, as they're known here, 'The Wilderness Years' – records have come easily to Brechin City. They were the first club to dabble in sponsorship, when the people of Brechin offered them money to go to play somewhere else.
It's Only an Excuse, BBC Radio Scotland spoof documentary, 1986.

You can kid yourself that what you're doing is of world importance, but there are more important things in life. For example, Brechin City might be relegated this year.
Celtic vice-chairman **David Smith**, who moved to Brechin when he was ten years old.

CELTIC

That Celtic team was like the old Labour Party. All the diverse opinions and attitudes and points of view all worked in a common aim. That's what made them successful and that's what made us successful.
Skipper **Billy McNeill** on Celtic's nine-in-a-row era, *Only a Game?*, BBC documentary, 1985.

He trains them the right way, and he gets them to do what they can do well. He merges them all together. They're all helping each other. It's a form of socialism without the politics.
Bill Shankly on Jock Stein's methods, *Only a Game?*, BBC documentary, 1985.

1970–71: Celtic nickname: The Tims.
1971–72: Celtic nickname: The Tims.
1972–73: Celtic nickname: The Bloys.
1973–74: Celtic nickname: The Bhoys.
Teething problems for the ***Rothmans Football Yearbook***.

Whereas Ibrox is a stately home, Parkhead is a down-to-earth people's palace.
Simon Inglis, *The Football Grounds of Great Britain*, 1987.

I walked out of the front door at Celtic Park, believing it was for the last time, without a single director coming in to see me and bid me farewell. The critical response to this usually goes along the lines of, well, Celtic gave you a testimonial match. What more do you want? I do not want to sound ungrateful, but on these nights the player being honoured pays for everything out of his cheque for long service. Out of my testimonial money in 1980 came Manchester United's expenses and everything else down to the payment for the ambulance staff on the night of the match. The club give you the hire of their ground for nothing, that is all.
Danny McGrain, *In Sunshine or in Shadow*, 1987.

When I eventually got to the front door, the commissionaire refused to let me pass until I had shown him my parents' tickets. And I was still the captain of the club at the time!
Danny McGrain, *In Sunshine or in Shadow*, 1987.

I feel I have been too long at Parkhead, and there is a vast difference in the ability of the players who have left and those who have come. I am not prepared to go through it all again next season, and I had hoped there would be plans to make the type of signing which will make a difference in challenging in Europe.
Tommy Burns submitting a transfer request, June 1984.

If it was up to me, our application to join the English League would be made tomorrow.
Manager **David Hay** after Celtic had lost the Skol Cup final to Rangers, 26 October 1986. Celtic had seven players booked and Maurice Johnston sent off.

Sometimes I wonder if Paul [McStay] might have made a better player if he had possessed a bigger ego, but I would never want to change him. I had a very healthy respect for people like Bobby Evans in the 1950s and then Paddy Crerand in the decade after that but, for awareness and skill, Paul is better than any of them, including Kenny Dalglish.
Celtic chief scout **John Kelman**, *Celtic Greats*, 1988.

I've publicly denied three times I'm leaving Celtic. I don't intend to go through my life denying it. I prefer to credit our fans with sufficient intelligence to see I want to stay.
Frank McAvennie, December 1988. He joined West Ham for £1.25 million in March 1989.

Graeme Souness, whatever Celtic supporters think of him, has done a brilliant job at Ibrox. If he hadn't come back to Scottish football and changed it all around, I wouldn't be at Celtic Park today.
Frank McAvennie, December 1988.

We allow laughing and joking, but we'll have no joviality.
Celtic coach **Frank Connor**, quoted by ex-Celt Mark McGhee, January 1994.

Paul McStay for Rangers? Sounds like a fair swap to me.
Letter in the _Sunday Mail_, 1992. Glasgow was being swept by rumours that Rangers were poised to bid for the Celtic skipper.

It's not a matter of money. I feel now is the time to explore the possibilities.
Paul McStay, May 1992. He later re-signed for Celtic.

I was told when I joined this club about Celtic's paranoia – now I know it's true. We are hard done by religiously and politically. There are people against us . . . I meet people who hate me just because I am the manager of Celtic.
Liam Brady, shortly after taking over at Parkhead, 1991.

It's a sad fact that Celtic have taken advantage of their top players. The kind of players who have supported Celtic and been really loyal to the club have been the ones who have suffered the most.
Charlie Nicholas, 1980s.

[Terry] Cassidy created more problems for Celtic in 22 months than anyone else since 1888.
Peter Rafferty, secretary of the Affiliation of Registered Celtic Supporters Clubs, October 1992.

The one that really put him under pressure, though, was Tony Cascarino. Celtic have never played with a massive target man, and Cas didn't go down well with the crowd. Buying him was a mistake which showed Liam never really understood the Celtic tradition.
Charlie Nicholas on Liam Brady, October 1993.

I should've had a bet on Tony Cascarino scoring for Chelsea. Everyone I've sold seems to score on their debuts – Andy Walker, Jacki Dziekanowski, John Hewitt and now Cascarino. What a Yankee that would've been.
Liam Brady, February 1992.

Enter an angel with a shamrock on her thigh
And a liking for great big monkeys with tears in their eyes
And she says, 'Come and see the Celtic,
You will love the way they play

But if this old team is to flourish
Don't kill McStay.'
Michael Marra's song, 'King Kong's Visit To Glasgow', 1993.

The name sounded good to me. Tough and exciting. I became a fan.
Dundee United boss **Ivan Golac** on how he became a Celtic supporter as a teenager in Yugoslavia, October 1993.

Let no one doubt the firmness of our resolve.
Rebel shareholder and ex-director **Brian Dempsey**, October 1993.

The club is now completely fractured. The board have no answers, no money and the supporters have no confidence in them. Even the staff at the ground have been wishing me luck. All I can say is, 'God help them'.
Fergus McCann, rebel leader, after being defeated in his bid to take over Celtic, November 1993.

We had a meeting with Tom Grant and Lou Macari, and Tom said he doesn't believe Cambuslang will ever happen. That's from the stadium director.
David Cunningham, Celts for Change, February 1994.

Classic confrontations that we've seen: Celtic against Inter Milan, Rangers against Moscow Dynamo, Aberdeen against Real Madrid, Gough against Roxburgh, Souness against Aggie the tea-lady at St Johnstone, and the Celtic board . . . against the rest of the world, really.
Only an Excuse '93 stage show.

I don't think you can afford to be flippant about things like this. If someone is motivated enough to make a call like that you have to believe they might take it further.
Director **Michael Kelly**, after receiving a death threat after the New Year's Day defeat by Rangers, 1994.

We're not on the right road and there's no point pretending we are.
Lou Macari after losing to Partick Thistle, 8 January 1994.

Most decent Celtic fans will be embarrassed by what Celts for Change are doing.
Celtic chairman Kevin Kelly, 10 January 1994.

Different managers have tried to correct it and it hasn't worked for them. It hasn't worked for Lou Macari yet either. I just don't think the whole thing is right.
Charlie Nicholas, 17 January 1994.

I am convinced that Gerald Weisfeld hasn't got a clue what he is letting himself in for. The last thing he wants is to get involved in Celtic. He doesn't realise the reality of Celtic Football Club. He's sitting over in Australia and he hasn't a clue what is going on. He had better come over here and face the music.
Fergus McCann as Weisfeld enters the Celtic boardroom battle, February 1994.

We have a situation where Celtic is going public. Shares are being purchased by we don't know who, underwritten by we don't know what, for the purpose of we're not sure.
Rebel leader and ex-Celtic director **Brian Dempsey**, February 1994.

I am not aware of any director who has sought a buyer for his current shareholding.
Vice-chairman **David Smith**, 25 February 1994.

This is nonsense. My first involvement with Smith regarding this [sale of shares] was a call from him.
Willie Haughey, 25 February 1994.

The only way to describe how we have been treated by David Smith is deceit and total betrayal. This man has led us up the garden path.
Willie Haughey of the Weisfeld consortium seeking Parkhead control, 25 February 1994.

Gefinor is the international company which is providing £20 million investment. The rest comes from grants.
Patrick Nally, managing director of Stadivarious, the marketing arm of Superstadia Ltd, 25 February 1994.

This kind of deal is simply not their [Gefinor] scene at all.
Keith Falconer of Martin Currie Fund Management Group, 25 February 1994.

In all their announcements, if you check six months later you find the reality is a different matter. This will be no different.
Brian Dempsey, 25 February 1994.

We've had no commitments and no agreements to finance any stadium or anything else in Glasgow.
David Hogan, executive of merchant bank Gefinor, 1 March 1994.

It is a diabolical situation. Someone isn't telling the truth.
Willie Haughey, 1 March 1994.

I didn't wake up that morning thinking that in a few hours I would be going into a meeting to stop Celtic Football Club going into receivership.
Brian Dempsey after he and Fergus McCann had saved Celtic, March 1994.

CLYDE

Clyde were the visitors to Easter Road and on a blackboard carried round the pitch was the message, 'Clyde Are Delayed'. No sooner had the bearer re-entered the stand than he came out again, together with the two teams. The game started and almost immediately Clyde scored. We could hardly concentrate on the game while we waited for the message to reach our part of the ground. It read, 'Clyde Have Arrived'.

Ian Wood, *The Scotsman*, 10 April 1989, quoting a letter on the pre-Tannoy era from James Bertram, St Ola, Orkney.

Wembley was just like Shawfield – after all, they have a dog track round the pitch there as well. The only difference was nobody was shouting 'Brown must go' at time-up.

Scotland assistant boss **Craig Brown**, August 1986.

When we were training on the pitch an announcement would come over the Tannoy telling us to get off because there were dog trials starting. They didn't want the ball hitting a dog. Many of the greyhounds had cost more than my players.

Scotland coach **Craig Brown**, recalling being manager of Clyde at Shawfield, October 1993.

CLYDEBANK

I got a signing-on fee of £20. Out of that I'd to buy a club blazer and flannels, which we all wore. That came to £16, leaving me £4 as a bonus for becoming a professional footballer.

Clydebank skipper **Jim Fallon**, October 1983, recalling signing for the club in February 1968.

We cannot demand fans have the correct attitude then let players get away with this.

Clydebank chairman **Jack Steedman** after Lex Grant and Davie Shanks were both sent off twice in a match against Clyde, 12 September 1987. The pair were transfer-listed and told they'd never play for Clydebank again. (Shanks was back in the team less than a month later.)

And I don't want to read any of that 'plucky wee Bankies' shite tomorrow. We had the chance to win when we were 3–2 up and didn't take it.

Clydebank coach **Jim Fallon** after his side lost 4–3 to Aberdeen, Scottish Cup fifth-round replay, March 1993.

When I was at Clydebank we'd a guy who went out to buy a loaf and went to Magaluf for a week. It was an end-of-season holiday and his wife had told him she didn't want him going on the trip. So he got up one morning, said he was away for a loaf, and never came back. All he took with him were the clothes he stood in and a plastic bag with a pair of shorts inside.

Former Bankies star **Davie Irons**, 1993.

COWDENBEATH

Football fans probably don't know it, but Central Park is world-famous in stock-car circles.
Cowdenbeath chairman **Gordon McDougall**, April 1992.

What I need in the First Division are people who want to play for me at Cowdenbeath on a chilly Wednesday night. Prima donnas won't do a thing for us where we're going.
St Mirren boss **Jimmy Bone**, June 1992.

You're always looking to win your home matches.
Boss **John Reilly**, after his side beat Queen's Park in the Scottish Cup at Hampden, December 1993. At the time, Cowdenbeath hadn't won a home match in 20 months.

Black Diamonds and the Blue Brazil [a book about the club] is peppered with the tragi-comic, the absurd, and the plain bizarre. Were you aware that Cowdenbeath once undertook a tour of Europe and played in front of 40,000 in Dortmund? Or they had an Egyptian centre-forward on their books in the 1920s? Or that in 1933 their manager quit to take over the hot seat at Manchester United? (a move which must have given rise to one of the most particularly unique CVs in the history of British football).
Archie MacGregor, *The Absolute Game* fanzine, January 1994.

DUMBARTON

Johann is thinking our offer over very carefully.
Dumbarton boss Sean Fallon, on the club's brave attempt to sign Dutch World Cup star Johann Cruyff, December 1980.

It is nice that a club in Scotland should be interested, but I still feel I can play at a higher level. This doesn't sound right for me.
Johann Cruyff, December 1980. It was later hinted that Cruyff was unaware the First Division in Scotland – where Dumbarton played – was not the top division.

At the beginning of last season I made the long trek to Boghead and was rewarded by the Sons going in at half-time 1–5 down to Berwick Rangers . . . In *The Absolute Game* issue 9 I had mentioned that there were some English lads regularly attending matches at Boghead. One of them had invited a number of his pals to the game with Berwick, clearly expecting the Sons to win. As the goals rained into the Dumbarton net in a truly extraordinary opening half-hour, the host stood grim-faced while his guests rolled about helpless with laughter. One of them announced to all and sundry that he had been watching Leeds United for 15 years but he had never had so much genuine entertainment crammed into 45 minutes in his life. Waving a fiver above his head, he declared that he was going to pay the gateman on the way out, as £2 was a completely inadequate amount to pay for such fun. Many of the Sons fans were unable to appreciate the humorous side of this.
Alastair McSporran, *The Absolute Game* fanzine, October 1990.

My teeth came out and bounced on the floor. I caught them and had them back in my mouth without missing a word.
Dumbarton boss Billy Lamont on a novel half-time team talk, May 1992.

DUNDEE

I have never done anything illegal. I have probably cut a few corners here and there. I probably left some blood on the table when I was younger.
Ron Dixon, February 1992.

On 29 January 1992 the bank sat in the boardroom and told us they were shutting the place down. They said that as of the following day they wouldn't cash any of our cheques and that they wanted the money owed – about £850,000 – in full. That was my first little surprise.
Dundee chairman **Ron Dixon**, August 1993.

We murdered them. We went for their throats and ripped them out. Teams have never asked questions about the Rangers defence. They just sit back. We showed what can be done if you are prepared to go at teams like Rangers.
Simon Stainrod after his side had beaten Rangers 4–3, August 1992.

If it had been a sunny day when we played Rangers I wouldn't have been wearing it. I am not only about flamboyancy.
Simon Stainrod remembering the fedora he wore for the Rangers game, January 1994.

I stand by every word . . . People said after that game that Andy Goram wasn't playing. My answer to that is his deputy, Ally Maxwell, cost more than the entire Dundee team.
Stainrod before the next meeting with Rangers, November 1992.

We achieved our minimum goal of staying up, but I don't believe you achieve the next step by gassing managers every 20 minutes.
Chairman **Ron Dixon**, June 1993.

I'm a guy who likes a challenge. I'm a guy who likes things that are difficult to do. When you combine that with a need for adventure, a desire to put something back into the world, a

love of sports, and a feeling that free enterprise can free men's souls, it's logical that I end up here and now, trying to do this.
Dundee's Canadian chairman **Ron Dixon**, eloquently explaining why he'd pumped over £5 million into the ailing Tayside club, August 1993.

We wasted a lot of money: £250,000 for Jim Leighton; £50,000 for Graham Rix; £80,000 for Paul Ritchie; £30,000 for Max Christie. It was money flushed down the toilet and we have nothing to show for it. But that happened because the place was being run by a clique.
Ron Dixon, August 1993.

Right you c**t, I understand you do impersonations of me. Let's hear it then.
Yorkshireman **Simon Stainrod** to *The Sun*'s Lindsay Herron, 1992. Stainrod later described the mimicry as 'very good'.

I'm not here to be eighth or ninth. My intention is to win the Premier League. If I didn't think it was feasible I wouldn't have spent £1 million on players this week.
Ron Dixon, August 1993.

I didn't realise how deep the dry rot at the club ran, but you don't run away at the first shot.
Ron Dixon, August 1993.

When he came to this club all he could say in English was 'Yes', 'No', and 'Morning'. A week later he'd added 'Thank you' and 'Budweiser'.
Dundee boss **Jim Duffy** on Czech defender Dusan Vrto, October 1993.

DUNDEE UNITED

Neil Paterson, Dundee United's amateur inside-left, 1936–37. During the second half of the season he was team captain, an honour almost equalled 23 years later when he won a Holly-wood Oscar . . . He believes he is the only Scots writer to have won the award – he is most certainly the only former Scottish league footballer!
Picture caption in **Mike Watson**, *Rags to Riches: the Official History of Dundee United*, 1985. Paterson won the 1960 Best Screenplay Oscar for *Room at the Top*.

It's dangerous to draw a line and say everybody below it is out of the Scottish League. In 1959 Dundee United were second bottom of the Second Division. Some people might have said then that they should go, that Dundee can't support two clubs, etc, etc. I think you've always got to allow for clubs 'recovering' themselves.
Bob Crampsey, *The Absolute Game* fanzine, October 1991. (United actually finished third-bottom in 1958–59.)

When I took over we'd two 'S' forms, Graeme Payne, who's now with St Johnstone, and Steve Mellon, who's now with the fire brigade. There were also three players – players, remember – at the club who were older than me – Doug Smith, Dennis Gillespie, and Davie Wilson.
Jim McLean, December 1986, recalling taking over Dundee United in 1971.

An absolute miracle.
Jim McLean on winning the 1983 title with a squad of 12 players, December 1986.

Later it was discovered that the club president had tried to make sure of victory against us by attempting to bribe the referee. The man in charge was a Frenchman, and a good, top-class referee, Joel Quiniou. Whatever happened, the money – and it was alleged to have been around £50,000 – never reached him. And he handled the game well. I still remember how he disallowed a goal from Bruno Conti when one of his linesmen

163

signalled that another player had strayed into an offside position. I was convinced that it was a good goal but he chalked it off and the president must have wondered what had happened to all his cash.

Richard Gough on playing against AS Roma in the European Cup semi-final for Dundee United, 1984, *Field of Dreams*.

Some of those who let us down have played their last game for us.

Dundee United boss **Jim McLean** after losing the Scottish Cup semi-final to Hearts, April 1986. (Within weeks Stuart Beedie, Davie Dodds and Billy Kirkwood all left Tannadice.)

I'm definitely maybe going to play Sturrock.
Jim McLean, 1986.

You can't expect supporters to turn up and watch pound notes laid out on the field. They want to see good players.

Dundee United chairman **George Fox**, August 1986.

To continue in the masochistic line I undertook an opinion poll of a sample of United fans, amounting to a grand total of four, as to which [Cup final] was the worst defeat. The consensus seemed to be the miserable 1987 Cup final against St Mirren. The rank awfulness of the Paisley team, the ugliness of the goalscorer and the part-time, never-to-be-seen-again nature of the St Mirren support combined to make that final a particularly black day.

Archie Cameron, *The Absolute Game* fanzine, August 1991.

It was the worst Scottish Cup final I had ever seen . . . the game was a disgrace, an absolute, utter disgrace.

Jim McLean on the 1987 Scottish Cup final, *Jousting With Giants*.

I would not expect an amateur team to lose the goals we lost.
Jim McLean after the 4–0 defeat by Royal Antwerp in the UEFA Cup, October 1989.

I don't smoke or drink, but I will make an exception if we win a trophy. I'll go back into the dressing-room and get blootered.
Freddy Van Der Hoorn, Dundee United's Dutch defender, 1990.

DUNDEE UNITED

RULES FOR ALL MEMBERS OF THE PLAYING STAFF
Shaving: Players are allowed one day's growth (management will make final decision on growth). *Fine*: £25, doubling if repeated.
Extract from the **Dundee United** code of conduct charter, January 1993.

Everything I have tried in my life has worked. This will, too. I am a very ambitious person. I believe it is a waste of time to be second.
Ivan Golac, October 1993.

I had other interests besides football. Music and nature, for instance. I had trained to be an agricultural engineer in Belgrade. I am interested in nature and, of course, music. If you can teach your children to love these two, you teach them to love life. I am fortunate we have succeeded in doing that with our daughters.
Ivan Golac, October 1993.

My wife and I walk in the country almost every night. The best thing, though, is a lovely open fire, Strauss or Jim Reeves playing, and a glass of wine in my hand. Having said that (some people) must be thinking, 'What is he talking about?'
Ivan Golac, October 1993.

We'll be looking to score at least three goals and I'm confident we can do it. Brondby are static at the back and vulnerable at set-pieces. They're cumbersome and square and have no real pace.
Dundee United boss **Ivan Golac** before his side met Brondby, UEFA Cup first round, first leg, 14 September 1993. Brondby won 2–0 and eventually knocked United out on aggregate.

We're like the Red Cross – if anyone needs a revival, we're around to help them. We were a joke. We must be in the Guinness Book of Records under 'Stupidity'. We were useless, a bloody disgrace. How can they be nervous when they're two goals up? That's the way amateurs react.
Ivan Golac after watching his side throw away a two-goal lead for the second time in five days, 13 November 1993.

DUNFERMLINE

He [Pat Stanton] also had permission to spend a staggering £43,000 on Aberdeen's Doug Considine. When Doug later left the club to work in a laundry the saying 'being taken to the cleaners' took on a whole new meaning.

Jim Leishman, *The Giant that Awoke*, 1990.

The evening before the Celtic match I had watched a TV documentary on Martin Luther King and I was moved by the man and his faith. It rubbed off on me because when I had my team talk I spoke of my faith in Dunfermline Athletic. I said that I too had a dream – to see the club back where we belonged. I made it funny, of course, by saying to the players just before they went out on the pitch, 'Do you believe?' They roared back, 'I believe! I believe!'

Jim Leishman on the team-talk before Dunfermline beat Celtic 2-1, August 1987, *The Giant that Awoke*, 1990.

He asked me for £500 to sign. I beat him down to £300, with the proviso I bought the next round of drinks – a pint of heavy for him and a Guinness for his girlfriend.

Dunfermline boss **Jim Leishman** on signing striker John Watson, who later scored 85 goals in just over 200 games, September 1991.

EAST FIFE

One of the East Fife fans had begun queueing at the refreshment stall when it was 1–0. By the time he had his chops wrapped around a mince pie it was 3–0 and his Saturday afternoon was becoming distinctly unenjoyable ... He roundly abused each of the Fife players in turn, reserving particularly venomous invective for the goalkeeper. By the time he got round behind the goal where the target of his spleen was 'minding the net', he had worked himself into a truly furious lather. He stood a few feet behind the custodian and verbally pitched into him in colourful terms, during which the phrases 'useless c**t' and 'f***ing wanker' featured prominently. When the ball was safely up the other end of the field, the hapless goalie left his line and went behind his goal and indicated to this individual that he was going to 'smash your f***ing face in'. Undaunted, the Fife fan gestured in the traditional outstretched arms fashion, saying, 'C'mon then, big man.' Unfortunately for fight fans the ball chose that moment to reappear in the vicinity of the Fife goal and the goalie had to sprint towards the edge of the box, shouting, 'After the game!'

Alastair McSporran, *The Absolute Game* fanzine, on East Stirling v East Fife, October 1990.

EAST STIRLING

My eye immediately fell upon a young full-back playing for
East Stirling and I realised here was a gem buried in the lower
regions of Scottish soccer. His name was Eddie McCreadie.
Trying not to look too concerned after the game, I approached
the East Stirling manager and asked him, in as casual a way as
I could, how much he'd take for him . . . Tentatively he
replied, 'Say £5,000?' 'Done,' I said . . . It was one of my best-
ever signings.
Tommy Docherty, *Call the Doc*, 1981.

There seems to be a true vinyl junkie at the helm in the Firs
Park music box. I've only been there a handful of times, but
I've already heard most of Television's *Marquee Moon*, a selec-
tion of Lee Perry's weird reggae, and some unidentifiable but
tasty blues.
Alastair McSporran, *The Absolute Game* fanzine, March 1990.

The club announced last week that our record signing John
Workman had been given a free transfer. The 26-year-old full-
back joined the club from Stranraer in October 1989 at a cost of
£2,000.
Extract from **'Shire match programme**, March 1992.

Clubs like ours live on handouts. The only businesses which
run on charity are Oxfam and Scottish football, but that's all
coming to an end. I give the club three years, if that.
'Shire director and chief shareholder **Alan Mackin**, after seeing plans for the
club thwarted by an outdated voting system, November 1992.

FALKIRK

Perhaps the fact that Syd Puddefoot was for several seasons a Falkirk player deserves special mention. By signing Puddefoot to strengthen their side soon after the War, Falkirk created quite a stir in Scottish football circles. Scottish clubs had usually been sellers of star players to English clubs at high fees, but in this case Falkirk went into the English 'market' and paid something like £5,000 for the man they wanted.
The Football Encyclopædia, 1934.

Even his mother calls him Yogi.
Falkirk assistant boss **Billy Brown** on Brockville defender John Hughes, February 1991.

The standard would surprise a lot of people down south. There aren't many English Second Division sides who'd get a kick of the ball at Brockville.
Falkirk striker **Simon Stainrod**, April 1991.

I must be the only person in the world to say no to Barcelona and yes to Brockville.
Simon Stainrod, April 1991. Stainrod turned down a seven-month loan deal to join Terry Venables at Barcelona in 1985.

When I look around the Premier League at the skilful players there are, I honestly wonder how I get a game in it.
Falkirk cult figure **Crawford Baptie**, November 1991.

I have too much respect for football to be involved with players who do nothing but tarnish it and the image of Falkirk.
Jim Duffy, resigning as Falkirk boss, November 1989, after players were involved in a nightclub brawl.

I got a phone call from a disco manager in Saltcoats about an incident that involved seven of them and I decided to suspend them all. But I had had a couple of problems with directors who I thought were interfering in my job and one of them said it would be best if two of the players weren't suspended. I knew what he meant, that these two were worth money and their market value might go down, but I felt I would be left with no credibility if that was how we did it. It [resigning] was a mistake. I should have just carried on, suspended them and got on with the job. I put it down to naivety, inexperience and just plain stubbornness.

Dundee assistant boss **Jim Duffy**, October 1992, on his reasons for quitting as manager of Falkirk in November 1989.

One of Cadette's strengths is holding off people with his back to goal. If that wasn't legal, nor were many of Kenny Dalglish's during his career.

Falkirk boss **Jim Jefferies** after Kevin Drinkell's goal against Rangers was disallowed because Cadette held off his marker during the build-up, 1992.

FORFAR ATHLETIC

Forfar Athletic can go back to 1885, and they have taken a very prominent part in the legislative side of the game in Scotland. Strangely enough the big honours of the game have eluded them.

The Football Encyclopædia, 1934.

At the meetings I go to, every manager bats for his own club. Nobody's for the good of Scottish football. We're all in it for 'us'.

Forfar manager **Doug Houston**, *Only a Game?*, BBC documentary, 1985.

HAMILTON ACCIES

One such is 'Fergie', who is Hamilton Accies' most famous fan. Most readers will have heard, or heard of, Fergie. He's a bit of a legend in his own lunchtime, mainly due to his foghorn voice which has been honed by years of selling evening papers on street corners. It's only a small step from bawling 'Awrahauftimescoresaniracin' to yelling 'Safuckincorneryablinbastartye' around the grounds of Scotland. On one occasion Fergie was in Perth to watch the Accies against St Johnstone. The Accies lost badly. After the game, the Hamilton team bus was on the road home when the driver spotted the lonely figure of Fergie trudging along in the dark trying to hitch a lift. The players unanimously decided to stop and pick the old bugger up. Ten minutes further along the road the bus stopped again and Fergie was forcibly ejected, having spent the intervening time slagging the entire playing staff for their woeful performance that afternoon, in a colourful language which is uniquely his own.

Alistair McSporran, *The Absolute Game* fanzine, April 1991.

Many people think that story is apochryphal, but it's absolutely true. We'd played at Brechin and Fergie had missed his supporters' bus back to Hamilton. It was pouring with rain and he begged us to take him on the team bus, or he'd have to hitch-hike home. We agreed but I warned him before he got on not to to say a word to anyone. He got on, the bus started, and he lasted about 10 seconds. He started with the directors, then the three women who were on the bus, and was about to start on the players when we stopped and threw him off. He'd been on the bus about 20 minutes. I can remember it yet. We left him outside a chip shop in Arbroath.

Former Hamilton secretary **Alan Dick** on famous fan Ian 'Fergie' Russell, March 1994.

We fully accept he gets carried away and does not know what he is shouting. He even swears profusely when denying he has been swearing. We tried putting him in quarantine in a

distant part of the terracing but that did not work either. He could still be heard all over the ground.
Hamilton managing director **David Morrison**, announcing a life ban on Fergie, March 1987.

We banned him for life in 1987 and he turned up for the next game with a ladder, propped it against the boundary wall, climbed up, and started shouting and bawling again.
Alan Dick, March 1994.

I know I get carried away at times but I don't do anyone any harm.
Ian 'Fergie' Russell, March 1987. (At the time of writing Fergie had been handed another life ban by Hamilton, but it does not seem to have diluted his fervour.)

I never finish buying players. I'm like my wife when I go out shopping. I never want to stop.
Hamilton boss **John Lambie**, August 1986.

They don't talk back. And if they did, you can always wring their necks.
Hamilton boss **John Lambie** on his pigeons, September 1986.

I wouldn't blame [Terry] Butcher. If it had been one of my players I'd have wanted him to go in the way Butcher did.
Hamilton boss **John Lambie** on the tackle which broke Hamilton's Bobby Barr's leg, January 1987.

As far as I'm concerned, the referee and his linesmen saw both incidents clearly and acted accordingly.
Hamilton's **Albert Craig** after Rangers' Graham Roberts and Ian Durrant were sent off for fouls against him at Ibrox, January 1987.

The chairman said on the bus going to Ibrox that if it went to a replay it couldn't go on at Douglas Park because of the new lights being installed there. I said, 'I suppose we'll just have to go and win it.'
Hamilton boss **John Lambie** after the team's Scottish Cup win against Rangers, January 1987.

I never spoke to the manager about it after the game. He just sat there in the dressing-room in a bit of a daze.
Hamilton's **Adrian Sprott**, after his goal at Ibrox knocked Rangers out of the Scottish Cup, January 1987.

Baptised 'Vodka Vic' by doting Hamilton fans, he will always be remembered at Shrewsbury as the player who overturned a team-mate's car on the way to buy a paper.
Stuart Cosgrove on Victor Kasule, *Hampden Babylon: Sex and Scandal in Scottish Football*, 1991.

Perhaps I will become a coach when I retire. I could start in Bothwell, where I live, and then go on to Hamilton Accies.
Oleg Kuznetsov, February 1991.

HEARTS

One of the leading clubs, the Heart of Midlothian, was responsible for founding a footballers' battalion of the Royal Scots in Edinburgh, and the Heart of Midlothian team, which was perhaps the best team they ever had, joined the regiment *en bloc*, and several of them made the supreme sacrifice.
The Football Encyclopædia, 1934.

It was like buying a shop with no stock when I bought the club . . . I never realised Hearts were in such a mess. I also never realised the extent of the responsibilities and pressure.
Wallace Mercer, *Only a Game?*, BBC documentary, 1985.

In the end it's a meaningless investment, because you can't own the heart and soul of a community.
Wallace Mercer, *Only a Game?* BBC documentary, 1985.

He was only ever put in the [manager's] position as a stop-gap appointment, but Tony [Ford] began to believe his own publicity. He went from painting the dressing-room to being a superstar who wore the white jackets and drank the gins.
Wallace Mercer, *Heart to Heart*, 1988.

Everybody's blood was hot at the time, and foolishly I had a wee slap at Provan as I released the ball. I nearly landed down beside him when I saw his reaction. He didn't fall to the ground – he threw himself on it as if he had spotted a tenner, then clutched his face and started groaning as if he had been attacked by a flame-thrower . . . The man's antics were deplorable. He was deliberately getting me sent off . . . Whatever anyone else thought, I knew my conscience was clear, but I wonder how Davie Provan can sleep at night.
Willie Johnston, *On the Wing!*. Johnston was playing for Hearts when the incident occurred.

If they play well against us, we go out and buy them.
Hearts boss **Alex MacDonald**, *The Boys in Maroon*, 1986.

Three times I tried to go in and say something that would lift them, but there was just no way. There was nothing that could be done to relieve the most hellish pain I had experienced in over 20 years in the game.
Alex MacDonald after losing the title in the last few minutes at Dens Park, May 1986.

This season belongs to Hearts, even if they finished without a trophy.
Aberdeen manager **Alex Ferguson** after beating Hearts in the 1986 Scottish Cup Final.

His leg looked like a pound of mince.
Alex MacDonald on Sandy Jardine's leg, injured during a tough Edinburgh derby, August 1986.

He'd been over the course before as captain of Motherwell. I didn't know anything about him as a player, but when he took a seat opposite me in the boardroom I noticed he had pale blue eyes and tight skin across the forehead. I thought he looked like a gunfighter.
Wallace Mercer on Stewart McLaren, *Heart to Heart*, 1988.

He has a ration-book of words and he doesn't want to use them all up at the one time.
John Colquhoun on Joe Jordan, 1991.

He gives you a row at the bottom of his voice.
John Colquhoun on Joe Jordan, 1991.

Salman Rushdie just phoned to tell me that I'm bad news and he doesn't want anything more to do with me.
Wallace Mercer after receiving a bullet in the post during his bid to take over Hibs, 1990.

They looked at my previous medical records and panicked, even though I'd had no knee problems at Dundee. The funny thing was, Hearts' doctor drove me back from the medical and asked me where in Edinburgh I planned to live and, in return, I asked his advice on some nice areas. He had spoken to the surgeon who had performed the previous operations and knew what had gone before, so for Hearts to then turn round and reject me after I'd had that conversation with the doctor just wasn't right. I don't know if it was a move by Wallace Mercer to try to buy someone in an attempt to please the fans. Whatever it was, I don't have any time at all for Mercer and he isn't one of my favourite people ... I know football is a business, but I still harbour a lot of resentment towards him.

Rangers defender **John Brown**, recalling the failure of a 1986 move to Hearts, 1993.

My expert advisers tell me that while you can put Rangers and Celtic guys together, who argue amicably about the merits of their teams, if you put a Hearts supporter like me in a cell alongside a Rangers supporter, it is a recipe for disaster.

Alan Bishop, chief inspector of Scottish prisons, February 1993.

I am a product of the Thatcherite '80s. Perhaps Hearts now require the softer approach of the '90s.

Wallace Mercer, December 1993.

HIBS

When we were playing teams the local bookmakers clubs would give three goals of a start to the opposition just to get a bet.

'Famous Five' striker **Lawrie Reilly**, *Only a Game?*, BBC Documentary, 1985.

When the idea of the European Cup came up, Harry Swan [Hibs chairman] jumped at it straight away. He was a very forward-looking man. He wanted smaller leagues in Scotland long before they arrived, and showed equal foresight when it came to mixing with the continentals.

SFA assistant secretary **Willie Allan**, *The European Cup, 1955–1980*.

When Hibs won the Drybrough Cup final against Celtic in 1972 I hauled Eddie Turnbull, the Hibs manager, out of a rejoicing dressing-room, still flushed with triumph, still rabbiting on about how splendid a victory it had been. We wired him up, got a voice level from him, got a countdown on the tape about to run to a recording when suddenly it dawned on him that he was about to be on television. 'How much am I getting for this?' he asked. 'I really have no idea,' I said. 'Well, you can stuff it up your arse then,' he replied, ripping off the mike and storming off up the tunnel.

Archie MacPherson, *Action Replays*, 1991.

If I wasn't the manager I'd have gone home early.

Boss **Alex Miller** after a 0–0 draw, 1992.

Keith Wright would be a tremendous player if he didn't have such a big chin. It obviously hampers his performance and was definitely the reason why we didn't hit it off straight away.

Darren Jackson on team-mate Wright, August 1993.

KILMARNOCK

There was a principle at stake as well as the integrity of the club to take into consideration.

Manager **Jim Fleeting**, sacking defender Kenny Brannigan after he was sent off after two minutes against Queen of the South, January 1989.

In the former's 'Personality Profile' [in the club programme], the unfortunate Gordon Wylde reveals himself to be a disaster area of previously unheard-of proportions. Recovering anyway from serious injury, the man has fallen through a plate-glass window, broken both arms, needed 18 stitches in an eye, and twice broken his nose.

Mike Alway, *The Absolute Game* fanzine, May 1990.

MEADOWBANK

I remember going through on the Meadowbank supporters' club bus to see them playing Queen's Park and they had some great chants, like 'Give us an F, give us an I, give us an S, give us an L, what's that spell, Thistle!'
DJ (and secret Meadowbank admirer) **John Peel**, February 1983.

He [Rick Wakeman] knew all the players. The first thing he said to me was 'The big lad from Alloa's playing well!'
Meadowbank boss **Terry Christie** on their celebrity fans, February 1983.

We have no scouts, no reserve team, and we've never signed a boy on 'S' form. My main sources of info as regards local talent are my two sons, Max, an under-15 Scottish schools player, and Kevin, who's 18 and playing for Salvesen Boys Club.
Terry Christie after Meadowbank clinched the Second Division title, May 1987.

In 1974 [when Meadowbank – née Ferranti – were admitted to the Scottish League], the poor communications argument had some validity, but the real objection then was two-fold, and it was led by the likes of Tom Fagan at Albion Rovers. First, you would have needed an overnight journey to go up there [the Highlands] in the winter. And the second, more potent, objection was that you were almost certainly going to get beaten. Whereas everyone thought that Ferranti were a soft touch. You came through – an hour on the motorway – you duffed up Ferranti and that was your pools money, and that paid your wages for another week.
Journalist **Bob Crampsey**, *The Absolute Game* fanzine, October 1991.

MONTROSE

Q: Were you happy at the prospect of coming to Links Park?
A: I was sweating with excitement. It didn't take me long to say 'yes' to the move, even though I'd never heard of Montrose.
Q: What was your first impression?
A: I thought I'd come to a chicken factory. It was also reminiscent of a Chinese women's volleyball team.
A peek into the surreal world of Montrose's Dutch striker **Ivo Den Biemen**, May 1991.

We played a closed-door game at Montrose. It wasn't at their ground but on what amounted to a public park. The state of the park was terrible and the game wasn't much better. I remember thinking, 'What kind of country have I come to?'
Aberdeen keeper **Theo Snelders**, recalling his first game for the Dons after his £300,000 move from FC Twente, July 1991.

Life's battles don't always go to the stronger or better man,
But sooner or later the man who wins is the man who thinks he can.
Montrose boss **Jim Leishman**, quoting Arnold Palmer before his side met Celtic in the Scottish Cup, January 1992. Montrose lost 6–0.

My sales manager was down at Ibrox. He came back with a lot of information about how they run things. Really and truly, they're not doing it any better than we are. They've just got a better team on the park.
Montrose chairman **Bryan Keith**, November 1993.

MORTON

The players will not get one penny. They embarrassed me, the club and the supporters.
Manager **Allan McGraw** after Morton's exploits in the Tennents Sixes, April 1988. (They lost 9–3 to Dundee and 4–1 to Aberdeen.)

I've checked the ball into a clinic in Switzerland for two weeks of recuperation after the battering it took . . . We deserved a replay, but if it was anything like this I'd be bored to tears.
Morton boss **Allan McGraw** after being knocked out of the Scottish Cup by Kilmarnock, February 1994.

MOTHERWELL

The final game [of Motherwell's 1928 South American tour] was a 5–0 defeat by a Brazilian select in Rio before a 40,000 crowd. Time being short, before their ship sailed, the Steelmen had to be hurried by taxi to the docks still wearing their football gear.

John Swinburne, *A History of the Steelmen, 1886–1986.*

Motherwell is one of the 'classic' teams of Scottish football. Throughout the country they stand in high esteem simply because of the touch of class they always try to bring to bear in their activities on the field of play. Not only that, but they have for long resisted tempting offers for some of their star players. It is, indeed, said that they turned down an offer of £12,000 for their great left-wing pair, Stevenson and Ferrier.

The Football Encyclopædia, 1934.

Had they but known, even greater forces were at work against Dundee in the shape of a cat by the stage name of Rhubarb. This had been the fictitious feline lead in an American film of the same name, starring Ray Milland, about a pussy possessed of paranormal powers used to inspire a baseball team to greater heights. The Motherwell coach, Ben Ellis, had been at the pictures in mid-January, before the Cup started, and hung a portrait of the screen character inside the dressing-room at Fir Park with the inevitable results.

Hugh Keevins and Kevin McCarra, *100 Cups: The Story of the Scottish Cup.* Motherwell won the Cup in 1952, the year concerned.

I stood up and was counted.

Roger Hynd on being sacked, 1978. He took Motherwell to the bottom of the Premier League in November 1978 – they were later relegated.

A man from Aberdeen wrote to say how much he'd enjoyed the game. But he made the point how hard it must have been for my wife Anne and daughter Julie, watching and wondering how I was. He enclosed a cheque for £10 so Anne could buy something for Julie while her dad was in hospital. Normally

I'd have sent it straight back, but he was so sincere I wrote back thanking him for thinking of us.
Goalkeeper **Ally Maxwell** after suffering severe internal injuries during Motherwell's Scottish Cup final win, 1991.

The way they [Motherwell] play will get the game stopped. All they want to do is defend. I doubt if I would pay to watch them. Not doing what they do against us, at any rate.
Rangers boss **Graeme Souness**, obviously not an admirer, *A Manager's Diary*, 1989.

There are times when I get far too much praise, which is an indictment of the state of the Scottish game. At Motherwell we have two sponsors' Man of the Match awards for each game. There have been matches when I've won one or the other and wondered what I'd done to deserve it. Then I'd think back and remember a flick here or a wee trick there and that's obviously what swung it my way.
Davie Cooper, March 1991.

My players thought they could come here and sneak a result. I thought their attitude was disgraceful.
Boss **Tommy McLean** after his side's first win at Ibrox in 14 visits, October 1993.

PARTICK THISTLE

I used to watch them wheeling like gulls, absorbed in their wonderful fitba'. They weren't in Africa or the Army any longer; in imagination they were running on the green turf of Ibrox or Parkhead, hearing instead of bugle calls the rumble and roar of a hundred thousand voices; this was their common daydream, to play (according to religion) either for Celtic or Rangers. All except daft Bob Brown, the battalion idiot; in his fantasy he was playing for Partick Thistle.

George MacDonald Fraser in 'Play Up, Play Up and Get Tore In' from *The General Danced at Dawn*, 1970.

Perhaps the most complicated magic routine of all belonged to a goalkeeper, Alan Rough, who publicly admitted that he went 'in fear of missing out some part of my match-day ritual'. The pattern went as follows:

1 He must not shave on match-day mornings.
2 He must carry a key-ring with a thistle motif.
3 He must also take with him to the ground an old tennis ball.
4 He must put in his pocket a miniature football boot he found in his goal-net one afternoon.
5 He must wear a small star-shaped medal.
6 He must always use peg number 13 in the dressing-room.
7 He must put on his original number 11 jersey, from the days of his first soccer club, underneath his keeper's sweater.
8 As he goes through the tunnel, he must bounce the ball off the wall three times.
9 When he approaches the goalmouth, he must kick the ball into the empty net.
10 Throughout the match he must blow his nose as many times as possible, using handkerchiefs tucked inside his keeper's cap specially for the purpose.

He concludes this formidable list by saying, 'I don't think I could play without going through these preparations. And nothing discourages me, not even a seven-goal hammering.'

Desmond Morris, *The Soccer Tribe*, 1981.

SCOTTISH FOOTBALL QUOTATIONS

Our defence couldn't keep weans out of a close.
Partick Thistle manager **John Lambie** after his side's 6–3 defeat of Dundee, August 1992.

John said, 'None of the players at Firhill have got everything. If they had, they wouldn't be at Firhill!'
Partick striker **Roddy Grant** recalling boss John Lambie's powers of persuasion, November 1993.

That's great. Tell him he's Pele and get him back on.
Partick boss **John Lambie**, on being told concussed striker Colin McGlashan didn't know who he was, 1993.

I'm not going to praise them. We were a disgrace in that first half. In the second half it was easy to look good. Ian Cameron may have got four goals but he needed a good kick up the arse before he started playing. And I can tell you that won't be the team for Saturday because it wasn't as good as the scoreline sounds.
Boss **John Lambie** after his side had beaten Albion Rovers 11–1 in the League Cup second round, 11 August 1993. It was the heaviest defeat in Rovers' history.

The boy could have went out with some dignity. Instead of that he's went out a cheat and a liar. But he'll get his turn for telling lies . . . He might get a bad injury or something like that. Hell mend him. For the lies he's told he deserves whatever he gets.
Partick Thistle boss **John Lambie**, July 1993, after defender Davie Irons signed for St Johnstone.

Davie Irons? He's a great bloke who did a magnificent job last season and I was understandably upset to lose him. But I wouldn't wish an injury on anyone. I've had a couple of nasty knocks myself during my career and it's not the sort of thing I could say.
John Lambie, September 1993.

If he wasn't my manager I would be happy simply to have him as a friend. I like everything about the man.
Chic Charnley on Lambie, November 1993.

When I arrived in September 1990, the club had a front door that looked like a back door, a shabby reception area, and was generally suffering from 30 years of neglect.
Partick Thistle chairman **Jim Oliver**, May 1992.

I will not get suspended this season. I am determined that it will not happen. People know that I boil over and then it is all finished in seconds. I never bear grudges and I am not involved in vendettas or that stuff. As soon as I have done something stupid I have regretted it. This time I am not going to do it.
Nine-times sent off, 49-times booked Partick Thistle midfielder **Chic Charnley**, November 1993.

I know we are the cuddly toy of Scottish football, but we would rather win and be less loved.
Thistle chairman **Jim Oliver**, February 1994.

QUEEN OF THE SOUTH

The Queen of the South shall rise up in the judgment with the men of this generation and condemn them.

LUKE 11:31, New Testament. The Palmerston side are the only football club mentioned in the Bible.

QUEEN'S PARK

The club grew out of the enthusiasm of some young men who amused themselves by kicking a ball in Queen's Park on Saturday afternoons. On July 9, 1867, these young men met and formed a club – annual subscription 6d., entrance fee 1s.
The Football Encyclopædia, 1934.

Before the 1870s were over a revolution had occurred. It began at a club called Queen's Park in Scotland, where an inventive brain introduced the novel idea of deliberately passing the ball to one of his team-mates. Instead of having to steal the ball from an enemy after it had been lost, a Queen's Park player would receive it as a gift from a friend. Kicking it back and forth between themselves, they threw the enemy into total confusion.
Desmond Morris, *The Soccer Tribe*, 1981.

The wise old men of Mount Florida knew
If the game was to flourish some changes were due
When the science of football emerged from the dark
It was due in the main to the men of Queen's Park
Crossbars and corners
Free-kicks and throw-ins –
The scientific game.
Michael Marra's song, 'The Wise Old Men of Mount Florida', 1991.

We are entertainment. My lads take you on such highs and lows it's untrue. They would have a cavalry charge in the 94th minute if they could.
Queen's coach **Eddie Hunter** after his side won 4–3 at Cowdenbeath, February 1994.

RAITH ROVERS

His (then-manager Bobby Wilson) fate was sealed in November however, when Raith endured the ignominy of losing 6–0 at the Commonwealth Stadium . . . Of all the embarrassments suffered over the years, becoming the victims of Meadowbank's record victory has to be the ultimate shame.
Gary Oliver, *The Absolute Game* fanzine, May 1990.

When we first saw him he was built like my pinkie. Now he's built like my index finger.
Raith boss **Jimmy Nicholl** on striker Steve Crawford, after the 18-year-old scored a debut winner against Dunfermline, November 1992.

RANGERS

A club, the Rangers Association Football Club, was formed, and as the funds in hand were 'nil', a sub round was made for the purchase of a ball.
The Football Encyclopædia, 1934.

Even now, 30-odd years down the road, when I turn into Edmiston Drive in the morning I still get that bit of excitement going through me.
John Greig, 1993.

That team didn't get the publicity for what they did. That may have been my fault because I hid behind the hard-man image, but over the piece every player except MacDonald and Miller played for Scotland. Jardine, Forsyth, Jackson and Greig all captained Scotland in that year.
Rangers boss **Jock Wallace** on his 1976 treble-winning side, *Only a Game?*, BBC documentary, 1985.

Jock Wallace handed me a dozen complimentary tickets and said, 'Bring your family along tomorrow, you're playing. Get a good night's sleep.'
Derek Johnstone recalling how Jock Wallace told him he'd play, as a 16-year-old, against Celtic in the 1970 League Cup final.

If I have to be unpopular with the players to earn their respect, so be it. Bob Paisley taught me something about this. We were sitting in a bar in Bangkok at the end of the season when he finished as Liverpool manager. I told him the players thought he was a miserable bastard. He said, 'You think I don't know that? That's the way I wanted it. The day this club has a manager that the players love is the day this club will get into trouble.'
Graeme Souness, September 1986.

I made up my shopping list, with a goalkeeper and a centre-half at the top. I knew from personal experience that Bruce Grobbelaar at Liverpool would fit the bill and be enormously popular if I could persuade my old room-mate Kenny Dalglish to let me have him. The alternative was to try for England's number one, Peter Shilton, or his deputy, Chris Woods. Dalglish said no; Southampton wanted £750,000 for someone older than me; but Norwich City surprised me by accepting my offer for England's next goalkeeper, Chris Woods.

Graeme Souness, *No Half Measures*, 1987.

At Ibrox the next day there were 42,000, three stands of blue against one of green – and the outpost of green was awash with the Irish tricolour. An awesome noise of defiance rose up from among them – and when the players came out the sound in the whole place was volcanic, totally deafening. Who says all-seaters damp down the passion? Not here – you felt the glory and the animal both stirring in your gut. The noise never seemed to stop; and the game kicked off at two hundred miles an hour.

Pete Davies, *All Played Out*, 1990.

There will be dressing-room doors and walls around Scotland glad to know I've gone.

Terry Butcher on leaving to become Coventry player-manager, 1990.

There are too many hammer-throwers in the Scottish League. I sign a world-class player and have him put out of action after a game and a bit. The League is too tough.

Graeme Souness after Oleg Kuznetsov's knee injury in his second game, October 1990.

I don't like U2, that's rebel music, Southern Irish. And Simple Minds – I found out that Jim Kerr was a Celtic supporter, so all my Simple Minds tapes, they went out the window.

Terry Butcher, 1990.

That isn't just a stadium – it's a weapon.

Hearts boss **Alex MacDonald** after his side played at Ibrox, 1980s.

The power of Rangers was brought home to me that afternoon. Because of the building of the new stand Aberdeen had to change in a Portakabin. Alex Smith admitted later some of his younger players were overawed by the sheer noise.

Walter Smith on winning the 1991 title on the final day of the season, September 1991.

[Rangers] players were banned from going out on the Thursday and Friday nights before games, which is far from a harsh order to follow. But I regularly broke it on a Thursday, and even the occasional Friday as well. I played against Hibs in October '89 with a terrible hangover. It turned out to be the last game I ever played for Rangers.

Midfielder **Ian McCall**, August 1991.

Somebody said to me the other day that the Souness–Smith partnership was the best thing that ever happened to Scottish football. Not true. The best move was that a change in the share balance allowed one man to control Rangers Football Club. First Lawrence Marlborough, using David Holmes as his chairman, and now David Murray have provided the driving force, and the financial resources, to make this club a major force in Europe.

Walter Smith, September 1991.

I met Lawrence Marlborough on Sunday, November 18, at two o'clock in my office, then on Tuesday the 20th, and we went public on the 22nd. I was informed that Robert Maxwell was interested and I said to Lawrence Marlborough I'd very much like to complete the deal today – and that's what we did.

David Murray recalling his takeover at Ibrox, 1993.

I think Graeme saw something in Robbo's character which he didn't like. Perhaps he had felt that during the bad times we had had, Robbo was not a player you could rely on totally when the chips were down. There was a lot of disharmony in the dressing-room around that time and maybe Robbo had to go so that we could achieve the camaraderie that now exists at the club.

Richard Gough on ex-team-mate Graham Roberts, *Field of Dreams*.

I didn't think his treatment of the younger players was right. He would give them stick and he would do it in a nasty kind of way. I didn't like it . . . nor the way he picked on others rather than accept blame himself when he got it wrong.

Richard Gough on Graham Roberts, *Field of Dreams*.

Rangers would be better off signing a bad player, like me. They could take me round the ground before the game and the fans could throw things at me.

Hibs striker **Tony Higgins** talking about Rangers' sectarian policies, *Only a Game?*, BBC Documentary, 1985.

I didn't go to Scotland to risk breaking other players' legs. I'm very much against this style. I'm expecting a very hot reception when I get back. I think I will be fired.

Danish defender **Jan Bartram**, criticising Rangers' tactics under Graeme Souness in a Danish newspaper, 1988.

Three different papers were there, and to suggest they all got the same things wrong is a lot to suggest.

Carl Albrechtsen, sports editor of *Ekstra Bladet*, March 1988, after denials of the above by Bartram and Rangers.

When I get the ball . . . I know that in two-tenths of a second I will have at least twelve stud marks on my ankles. I just kick the ball up the field without looking

Jan Bartram quitting Scottish football, May 1988.

Your fitness definitely does have to be that bit higher to play for Rangers.

Graeme Souness, *A Manager's Diary*, 1989.

I offered Walter [Smith] the job before I asked Graeme to leave and that says it all as far as I'm concerned.

David Murray, 1993.

Why won't people believe us when we say no? We're fed up hearing the same question – everyone seems to know more than us. Where are they getting their info from?

Rangers assistant boss **Archie Knox**, asked about the club's plans to re-sign Trevor Steven from Marseille, July 1992. He was signed for a Scottish transfer record of £2.4 million the following morning.

We've done well, but if there was a league for drinkers we'd have won it by Bonfire Night.

Ian Durrant after Rangers won their fifth successive title, May 1993.

They didn't tell me it was a sumo wrestler's. I think they gave me his chins and stomach.
Andy Goram recounting how a donor's achilles had been used to replace his knee ligaments, *A Question of Sport*, October 1993.

It has become obvious to me at Rangers that the best players are the most difficult to handle. I think it's just human nature. If you're talented, if you have something special, it seems to be you are more delicate to deal with. Surely this is the case right across life's spectrum.
Walter Smith, October 1993.

In some ways I would say Rangers are an even bigger concern than AC Milan. For a start, Rangers own their stadium and it is one of the finest in Europe. Milan don't.
Ex-AC Milan striker **Mark Hateley**, *Top Mark!*, 1993.

In the middle of the park we have Ian Ferguson, who, apart from being good enough to get into most clubs, would surely be able to moan his way into whatever team he wanted to play for.
Mark Hateley on his Ibrox team-mate, *Top Mark!*, 1993.

Rangers are the only club I know of in Britain which insists on the players wearing a collar and tie to training. It's a wee bit classy and it shows you're ready for business.
Ally McCoist, February 1994.

My son was christened Alistair Ian Butcher. He's named after McCoist and Durrant, which means he's a cert to be a crackpot.
Terry Butcher, February 1994.

ST JOHNSTONE

All the credit must go to Geoff Brown. Without him McDiarmid Park wouldn't exist, the club would probably still be in the Second Division and we wouldn't be signing ex-World Cup stars like Sergei Baltacha and John McClelland.
Saints boss **Alex Totten**, July 1992.

Murderers and rapists have had a better press than me since I sacked Alex Totten.
Chairman **Geoff Brown**, January 1993.

Mark Hateley goes on the park and says, 'I will perform to my standards no matter who we are playing.' My lot want to pick and choose their games and that's not on. I called them mental cowards in the dressing-room at Motherwell before I made my feelings public. All I could see were heads looking at feet.
Saints boss **John McClelland**, November 1993.

ST MIRREN

It [St Mirren] was formed in 1876 by 15 rugger players who changed over to soccer a year later.
The Football Encyclopædia, 1934.

I am appalled that a St Mirren captain should behave this way. This type of action by any St Mirren player is not good enough for the club.
Saints boss **Alex Miller** after Billy Abercromby had received three red cards against Motherwell, October 1986. (The first was for a flare-up with Steve Kirk, the second for dissent, and the third after he'd left the pitch.)

I apologise to the supporters, my family, and the players' families for our performance.
St Mirren boss **Tony Fitzpatrick** after losing 5–1 at Dunfermline, October 1989.

You've got to say, 'no more'.
Manager **David Hay**, putting Chic Charnley up for sale two days after his third ordering-off of the season, February 1992.

I knew my days were numbered when I was warming up behind the goal at Parkhead one day and one of our fans shouted, 'Kinnaird, we like the Poll Tax more than we like you.'
Partick Thistle winger **Paul Kinnaird** reflecting on playing for St Mirren, 1992.

Ask yourself: could a rational adult watch a team lose three Scottish Cup semi-finals in a row and turn up for the next year's third-round tie with any vestige of hope? Could he persistently overlook the fact that this club actually sacked Alex Ferguson? Can he put from his mind the success Aberdeen went on to have with a team built around so many ex-Saints? Can he place faith in an organisation that sacked Fergie's successor because one of the directors' wives objected to his use of 'industrial language' during training? And that sacked the next man along, two days after winning at Parkhead? And that, when faced with the opportunity to appoint either Gordon McQueen or Archie Gemmill as manager (or even both, the former as assistant), chose a man who was so ambitious he had just spent the last twelve years with Stirling Albion? Could he support a team that lost the Renfrewshire Cup final on penalties to a Morton side that in the preceding weeks had managed to miss eight of the bloody things in a row?

Chris Brookmyre, The Absolute Game fanzine, March 1992.

All the talk about the danger of Ireland is rubbish. Paisley is more dangerous than the Province.

Coleraine (and ex-Saints) striker **Mark McWalter**, August 1993.

STENHOUSEMUIR

'Polish Cap Joins Stenhousemuir'.
Weekly News headline, 19 August 1978, recounting the unlikely tale of how
the Warriors had indeed signed **Marek Straczynski**, a twice-capped
Gwardia Warsaw striker who'd moved to Scotland to work as a refrigeration
engineer. He played only two games for them.

Our company only sponsor the arts. I don't think Stenhousemuir could be regarded by any stretch of the imagination as
artistic.
Prudential Insurance spokeswoman, turning down request from Warriors
fans for the company to sponsor them to compensate for TV ad containing
the line 'Stenhousemuir 1 Arbroath 7', 1992. An outcry followed, the company
apologised and sponsored a match.

STIRLING ALBION

It was so one-sided there were times during the second half when I wasn't really enjoying what I was watching. I'd told the players at half-time not to let up because we were five up. I reminded them our fans had paid to see 90 minutes' play and that they deserved their money's worth. But when my players began to chase records it became a bit of a farce.

Stirling boss **Alex Smith** on his side's 20–0 Scottish Cup win over Borders amateurs Selkirk, 8 December 1984.

I didn't even get the match ball. Stirling felt the Selkirk keeper, Midge Taylor, should get it. After all, he touched it more than anyone else.

Stirling striker **Davie Thompson**, scorer of seven goals against Selkirk, December 1984.

My abiding memory concerns our goalkeeper Midge Taylor. He'd just bought a new Lada car and when he woke up on the Sunday morning somebody had stolen the licence plates.

Selkirk boss **Jackson Cockburn**, recalling the Stirling match, December 1993.

Our centre-forward that day, Danny Munro, is adamant he got more kicks of the ball than anyone in our team because he had to kick-off so often!

Selkirk boss **Jackson Cockburn**, December 1993.

Perhaps an even more graphic illustration of Smiffy's [Alex Smith] unique talents as a manager comes from the astonishing fact that during the 90 minutes of a Scottish Cup tie against mighty Selkirk in 1984, the Binos scored more goals [20] than they had over an entire season [18] three years earlier.

Darren Park, *The Absolute Game* fanzine, October 1993.

I was ready when Stirling appointed me. My apprenticeship was certainly long enough.

Stirling boss **George Peebles** on becoming a manager for the first time at 50, February 1988.

STRANRAER

The Stair Park rabbit, a regular spectator during the 1985–86 season, seems to have gone AWOL of late.
Archie McGregor, *The Absolute Game*, fanzine, April 1988.

Fergie had years of frustration at Old Trafford until everything started to come right for him. And we know that feeling at Stranraer . . . United are the side that everyone wants to emulate and we're no different. They are encouraged to play with two, three, or even four men up front. They'll have Eric Cantona and Mark Hughes as their strike force, with Ryan Giggs and Andrei Kanchelskis out wide in support. We also use three men up front: Tommy Sloan, Lex Grant and Darren Henderson.
Stranraer boss **Alex McAnespie**, former Ayr United team-mate of Alex Ferguson, on the similarities between him and the Manchester United boss, February 1994.

THIRD LANARK

What did for Thirds [Third Lanark] was their chaotic share structure. They were the old athletic section of a territorial regiment (Third Lanark Volunteer Reserves), and they were funded, if that's the right word, by 700 to 800 folk, hardly any of whom had more than £20-worth of shares. So what happened was that a particularly grasping and predatory chairman simply read the obituaries in the *Glasgow Herald* and compared them with the list of shareholders and then went round and said to the widow, 'Sorry John's gone. You won't want to be bothered with the financial details – I'll give you a good price for the shares'. Which in fact he did and emerged a few years later as the majority shareholder.

Bob Crampsey, *The Absolute Game* fanzine, October 1991.

Bailie [James F.] Reilly attributed the club's present difficulties to rising costs, in particular to the cost of rebuilding their grandstand. There have been, however, other more important factors of which other, even larger, more prosperous football clubs might take note. For years now the club has been bedevilled by boardroom battles and mismanagement, both of which have militated against the creation of an efficient, let alone outstandingly successful, football team.

Glasgow Herald leader on Third Lanark, 8 June 1967. The club were unable to resume playing the following season.

£££

They [Rangers] had first to pass through a troubled adolescence, however, before reaching the commanding position of their maturity. During 1882–83 their president, George Goudie, had been required to loan £30 to the club to ensure its existence for a little longer, and even at the end of the season the wolf was, if not at the door, at least in the neighbourhood, with Rangers still owing £100.
Hugh Keevins and Kevin McCarra, *100 Cups: The Story of the Scottish Cup*, 1985.

Rangers paid the players bonuses every six months and when the end of the season came round I'd accrued around £1800. It was a considerable sum of money for an 18-year-old and I remember proudly clutching the envelope Scot Symon gave me stuffed with £20 notes.
Sandy Jardine, *Score and More*, 1987.

The salary at that time for being Scotland manager was £7500 a year – which wasn't a lot – and a car. At the start, I was writing for a local newspaper and I was getting paid as much by them as I was by Scotland.
Tommy Docherty, *Call the Doc*, 1981.

I asked the manager to enquire. He said there would be none and was surprised I'd asked. But I said, go on, just see. I've just heard the answer. No fee at all, but we might be able to keep a pullover each. Big deal.
Graeme Souness of Sampdoria, describing the reaction to asking for a fee for modelling Italian sweaters for *Vogue*, 1982.

Bobby Robertson cost us £70 and he's the team captain.
Dunfermline boss **Jim Leishman**, November 1986.

I'm not in a position to save. My earnings go to support my family.
Celtic's **Brian McClair**, January 1987.

I remember the entire Hearts board went along to Lesser Hampden to watch Malcolm Murray make his debut for the club in a reserve game as a trialist. It was a freezing cold night and we all had to make the decision as to whether the player was worth the money (£1000 and a testimonial game in Buckie). It was hard to envisage a situation five years on where I would be able to sanction an investment of £600,000 in new players.
Wallace Mercer, *Heart to Heart*, 1988.

I don't fine players because at this level, on our wages, hitting them in the wallet only penalises wives and children and I don't want that on my conscience.
Swindon boss **Lou Macari**, 1988.

I have always harboured the ambition to be the darling of the stockmarket.
Dundee chairman **Angus Cook**, announcing plans to float the club on the Stock Exchange, September 1989.

When you are innocent even the fine of one penny would have been a penny too much.
Lou Macari after being fined £1000 for his part in a betting scandal – referred to as 'a foolhardy misdemeanour' by the FA – at Swindon, February 1990.

The most sickening own-goal I've seen was by Scott Nisbet against Sparta Prague. I could have cried when it went in because we were on really big bonuses.
Former Ibrox striker **John Spencer**, 1991.

I have no problem with the mercenary tag. I'm a professional footballer and I expect to be paid for doing my job just like anyone else.
Frank McAvennie, January 1993.

He was slamming doors and banging drawers shut. We just watched the performance.
SFA commercial executive **Bill Wilson**, recalling the behaviour of the French FA's negotiator, Jean-Claude Darmon, over the SFA's demand for the £650,000 the French association had received from TV for coverage of the March 1989 Scotland v France World Cup tie, January 1994.

If you have the guts and are prepared to see these people in hell, you can fight them.

Former SFA secretary **Ernie Walker**, on the same negotiations, January 1994.

I kept on expecting to find a horse's head in my bed.

SFA commercial executive **Bill Wilson** on the TV negotiations with the Italian FA over coverage of the 1992 World Cup match, February 1994.

REFEREES

The referee is the 'king's eye' and the king is the Scottish Football Association, to whom your remarks to the referee, should they savour at all of disrespect, will be most assuredly reported. **SFA annual**, 1881–82.

Queen of the South had never beaten Rangers on their own ground. The score was 1–1 and near the end of the match there was a corner-kick. I was at the far post and I said to the ref, 'How long is there to go?' He said, 'You're all right, it's time-up after the kick.' The ball was kicked and it was an inswinger. Queen of the South had a big six-foot chap from Luncarty with a bald head called Jim Paterson. Up he went with the head, right into the back of the net, and I thought, 'Oh God.' There was a tremendous roar, which suddenly was silenced. The ref was pointing for a free-kick. George Young kicked the ball up the field and that was time-up.

Now the point of the story comes two years afterwards when I was privileged to attend a presentation at a lodge for that referee and as he made his speech of thanks he said that in 18 years of football he had never refereed a losing Rangers team. Now whether that was of any significance or not, I wouldn't like to say . . .

Former Ibrox goalkeeper **Bobby Brown**, *Glasgow Rangers Revisited: A 120-Year History*.

The day before the match I received a surprising telephone call asking me to find two linesmen to take with me to Scotland. They had forgotten to appoint any. I got hold of Jimmy Cattlin, from Rochdale, and my younger brother Frank, who was then officiating in the Yorkshire League. Frankly, some of the organisation in the early stages of the European Cup smacked of a chip-shop approach.

English ref **Arthur Ellis** recalling Hibs' first European tie, against Rot-Weiss Essen in October 1955.

On one occasion he felt aggrieved by decisions given by referee David Syme. As the latter came up the tunnel at the end of the

game expecting the worst, the gigantic figure merely muttered, 'Well done, son.' As the bemused referee moved away came the follow-up. 'Your father would have been proud of you.' The reference was to David Syme's father Willie, also a Grade I referee who had, in Stein's eyes, been equally hard on Celtic.
Bob Crampsey, *Mr Stein*, 1986.

Over-inclined to dive when tackled and far too prone to nark at the man in the middle. I recall booking him at Perth in the 88th minute when he played for Dundee. With St Johnstone well ahead he suggested the game should be abandoned because of a very light fog! His approach, I may add, was far from polite.
Ex-referee **David Murdoch** on Gordon Strachan before the 1982 Scottish Cup final.

I can't say anything about the match officials otherwise I wouldn't play or manage in Scotland again.
Graeme Souness after Rangers had both lost at Dunfermline in the Scottish Cup, February 1988, and had John Brown sent off in controversial circumstances.

The challenge by Bonner wasn't cynical. At no time did it cross my mind that a red card should be shown.
Ref **Bill Crombie**, *Scotsport*, April 1991, on a controversial Pat Bonner tackle on Eoin Jess at Pittodrie the previous day.

I can't remember a referee ever speaking out in this way. It's against the rules.
League secretary **Peter Donald** on Crombie, April 1991. The referee was later censured and warned as to his future conduct by the League.

There is nothing specific in the SFA's Articles of Association to prevent club officials speaking out regarding referees. It is inaccurate to say we don't like people talking about the game. However, the SFA controls football in Scotland. We support the promotion of the game, as long as that falls between acceptable parameters. From time to time, these parameters are breached.
SFA secretary-designate **Jim Farry**, January 1990.

When last Sunday's ref called me over and said, 'OK, Trevor,' at first I thought he was trying to wind me up.

Terry Butcher on being booked by Kenny Hope in his first Old Firm game, August 1986.

They say a good ref should always know where the ball is. I've shown just how it's done.
81-year-old ex-ref **Ned Shirley** of Troon after winning £108,000 on 'Spot the Ball', September 1986.

I've never seen a player with such a look on his face. From the very first minute, his eyes were glazed.
Ref **Howard King**, on sending off Chelsea's **Doug Rougvie** against Wimbledon after 22 minutes, December 1986.

It was a case of handbags at five paces and he was unlucky.
Chelsea boss **John Hollins** on Rougvie's role in the incident, December 1986.

You better ask the refs. It's them who keep booking him.
Rangers assistant manager **Walter Smith**, asked whether Graham Roberts was due a suspension, February 1987.

I don't think it would be advisable for Mr Syme to come anywhere near Airdrie for some time. That's judging by the number of calls I've had today about the decision.
Airdrie chairman **George Peat**, September 1991. Referee Syme's 87th-minute penalty award – later shown to be outside the box – had given Dunfermline an equaliser in the Skol Cup semi-final the day before, and the Pars won on penalties.

Brian [McGinlay] began by telling us of the occasion when the Central Scotland traffic polis had sneaked up on him and stopped him for drink driving. The following week he was refereeing an Old Firm encounter. At one point Ian Ferguson hit a shot past the post which Fergie clearly believed had struck a Celtic player on the way through. McGinlay awarded a goal-kick, much to Fergie's dismay. He remonstrated with McGinlay thus: 'Hey you, ya c**t. Ye no' f***in' see that?' While this amiable conversation was taking place, Super Ally was lurking in the background and he chipped in with, 'No f***in' see that? He couldnae even see a big white motor wi' a blue flashin' light on the top!'
Alastair McSporran, *The Absolute Game* fanzine, December 1992.

REFEREES

I read a bit about a referee being chased along the Gallowgate by fans . . . and that was in 1890. People are always looking back and imagining things were better. We Scots are particularly guilty of it.

SFA Refereeing and Education Development Director, **George Cumming**, February 1994.

OFFICIALS

A pillar of the church, a model of rectitude and, not to labour the point, a pompous pain in the neck.
Jim Baxter on SFA secretary Willie Allan.

The ball belongs to us and if it doesn't turn up we will take steps to see that it does. There is no question of the SFA turning a blind eye to the incident . . . if we ignore the business, then it would be a case of the law of the jungle taking over.
SFA secretary **Willie Allan** in a letter to Rangers after Jim Baxter left the field after the 1963 Scottish Cup final replay against Celtic with the match ball, intending to present it to team-mate Ian McMillan, who was soon to retire.

There was no game of football here today. We found ourselves on the field with cheats and cowards and we were associated with the scum of world football.
SFA secretary **Ernie Walker**, after the World Cup tie against Uruguay during the Mexico World Cup, June 1986.

It's like asking Frank Sinatra to take to the stage of the London palladium, knowing rocks were going to be thrown at him.
SFA secretary **Ernie Walker** on coin-throwing incidents at Ibrox, January 1987.

The spokesman for any organisation has a tendency to become associated with that body's statements. If that leads to me becoming unpopular, so be it.
SFA secretary designate **Jim Farry**, January 1990.

We're fed up with managers using clichés like 'I want players to die for me'. This is language more appropriate to a war zone than a sporting occasion.
SFA Chief Executive **Jim Farry** after eight orderings-off on the first day of the season, 1990.

In matters of discipline we've come to accept at Rangers that we're treated differently.

Graeme Souness, October 1990, after his presence on Rangers' Skol Cup final lap of honour, while he was serving a touchline ban, had angered the SFA.

Members feel they have been vilified in the press in the past.
Jim Farry, announcing a ban on pressmen attending council meetings, May 1991.

The main reason is the total ignorance of so-called professional players. They obviously don't know the laws of the game.
Jim Farry after 16 players had been sent off in the first week of the season, August 1991.

Referees are following rules made by men who don't pay to watch football. Those rules are ruining the game for those who do.
St Mirren boss **David Hay**'s view of the same subject, August 1991.

We wouldn't sanction anything critical of the referee's decision.
League secretary **Peter Donald**, refusing to allow the *Daily Record* to show a TV still picture of the Davie Syme penalty decision which so infuriated Airdrie in the Skol Cup semi-final, September 1991.

He [then-secretary of the Scottish League, Jim Farry] said that if it was up to him personally I wouldn't be allowed to play.
Dundee assistant boss **Jim Duffy**, October 1992, recalling his 1990 bid to re-start playing after having quit through injury in 1987.

The way professional players, for instance, are excluded from the running of football is disgraceful. It's a joke. We actually feel there is positive discrimination against ex-players. At some of these coaching courses you're frowned upon.
PFA chairman **Pat Nevin**, February 1994.

THE PRESS

Fans with typewriters.
Daily Mail reporter **J. L. Manning**, on Scottish football journalists, 1950s.

I always felt that was rather a nice way to describe us. I am a supporter with a typewriter. You can't travel round the world with Scotland just sitting there watching and reporting. You want them to win. You're there supporting them.
Journalist **Ian Archer**, *Only a Game?*, BBC documentary, 1985.

There are some journalists who have been involved in football for a long time and know what they're talking about and there's others who haven't got a clue.
Brian McClair, February 1986.

The Scotland squad in particular is always influenced by journalists. The manager is limited by the number of matches and players he can watch.
Brian McClair, February 1986.

Wee [Jimmy] Sanderson, he was the biggest. If Sanderson said you had a bad game, even if you thought yourself you'd done well, everyone believed him. Everything he said was gospel.
Paul McStay, February 1986.

There was the uncomfortable fact that matches between them [Rangers] and Aberdeen have not been celebrations of brotherhood and joy of late and the outlook for this one suggested that we were in for what is known euphemistically in the trade as a 'tight game'. Which means that two teams are going to spend the afternoon knocking lumps out of one another on the way to a goalless draw. But, to use another trade term, it's a funny old game and out popped a classic.
Ian Wood, *The Scotsman*, October 1987, after the Skol Cup final.

One caller rang in with an impressive opening gambit. 'Mr Sanderson, I haven't been to a game for years because fitba' nowadays is a load of crap.' (Sounds of Jimmy spluttering with fury at the other end of the line.) 'Mr Sanderson, I'd just like to ask you when you last paid to get into a football match.' (Jimmy's blood-pressure audibly sky-rocketing as he fumbles for a convincing reply.) Taking advantage of the wee man's temporary discomfiture, the caller delivered the *coup de grâce*: 'Mr Sanderson, I widnae pay you to sell newspapers never mind write the bloody things.' (Strangled squeals from the tranny, Jimmy apoplectic and incandescent with rage, Richard Park on the phone to the nearest psychiatrist, listeners staring with amazement as the wireless explodes.)

Alastair McSporran, *The Absolute Game* fanzine, August 1991.

Football in Scotland is fortunate to attract such high standards of journalism. Of course, there are times when sensational headlines do distort the facts, but I understand the pressure on the tabloids to come up with a never-ending stream of new angles. And over the piece, the coverage is excellent.

Wallace Mercer, *Heart to Heart*, 1988.

Rangers command more media attention than any other club in Britain. Oh, miles more than Liverpool. They don't have national papers on their doorstep twice a day. The Scottish papers know that something about Rangers on their back page, or even better the front page, will sell copies. It's just like Italy.

Graeme Souness, 1989.

Scotland fans never make trouble, they always enjoy the matches with their songs, dancing and bagpipes. One of them told us of the Scottish supporters' character: 'We never get cross with anybody, even if we lose. We are here to enjoy the game, and we always behave happily and cheerfully in front of other people but . . . we cry alone at home.'

Japanese newspaper **Mainichi** on the Tartan Army, June 1990.

Playing a game without flourishes or tactical plan, banking primarily on their will, the Scots permanently forced the Swedes to remain a very long way from their goal. The latter had been taken by surprise in the 11th minute by a goal by Stuart McCall; a magnificent introduction to a match which, unfortunately, as matters proceeded, was to degenerate to the point of resembling a caricature of football.

French writer **Dominique Grimault** on Scotland v Sweden in the Italy World Cup, *Italy World Cup 1990: The Great Moments*.

I've been reading your stuff over the last couple of years and it seems to me that you are just a little socialist.

Graeme Souness banning the *Glasgow Herald*'s James Traynor from Ibrox, November 1990. Traynor had been critical of Rangers' European record after they'd been beaten by Red Star Belgrade two days before.

Some of them are just anti-Celtic. But the same buggers would be queuing up to get on the gravy train if Celtic were back riding high. And wouldn't they be hurt if they weren't allowed on board. If we won the Scottish League, the Cup, the Skol Cup, and Europe, even the 400m sprint in the Olympics just now, these people would complain that we didn't win the breast-stroke.

Celtic chief executive **Terry Cassidy** on the press, January 1991.

Journalists are irrelevant. It doesn't matter what they say.

Celtic chief executive **Terry Cassidy**, 1991.

It was a weird trip. Chelsea won the game and each of us were awarded a small medal to polite applause from the locals. The losing side were presented with a trophy bigger than their centre-half, and to frenzied celebrations, at that. I have often wondered what kind of score the local journalists invented for the next day's papers and what version of events the nation was treated to that morning.

Pat Nevin, recalling a Chelsea trip to play Iraq in Baghdad, February 1994.

If I see one of your photogrphers there, I'll wrap his camera round his f***ing neck.

Ayr's **Hugh Burns** not issuing an invitation to his forthcoming wedding to *The Sun* newspaper, February 1994. (The paper had followed his strife-torn private life – Burns left girlfriend Kay McGaffney when she was 37 weeks pregnant, but later returned to her and daughter Hannah – with interest.)

OOOPS . . .

I was still quite young at the time and Peter McCloy looked so big in the Rangers goal that I was determined to get a good powerful strike on the ball. I managed that all right. I hit the ball so hard it not only went over the bar, but over the back of the terracing and out of the ground into the playground of Tynecastle High School.

Eamonn Bannon, recalling an unsuccessful October 1978 penalty for Hearts against Rangers, January 1984.

We felt we had to be level by half-time and big Alex's lob put us there. He'd scored a goal just like it in Cruden Bay training a couple of days before and one of the boys had shouted at him, 'Big man, you'll never do that again in your life.'

Willie Miller on Aberdeen's equaliser in the 1982 Scottish Cup final against Rangers.

When you're down in Largs for a couple of weeks and it's your night off you make your own entertainment. That's what we did.

David Hay recalling Jimmy Johnstone's maritime adventure, *Only a Game?*, BBC documentary, 1985. Johnstone was pushed out into the water late at night. He was in a rowing-boat equipped with only one oar, and after various haphazard attempts by team-mates to rescue him, the coastguard was called out to bring him back to shore.

He [Johnstone] couldn't get back in, but he was singing his head off. He was getting further and further away. Then two players, who shall remain nameless, started to paddle out to get him and the boat had a hole in it and started to sink.

Sandy Jardine on the same incident, *Only a Game?*, BBC documentary, 1985.

Wee Jinky Jimmy, boy, could he dribble. He couldn't row, but boy, could he dribble.

Only an Excuse '93 stage show.

Goodness knows what Graeme Souness will say when he gets home.

Rangers striker **Robert Fleck**, June 1986, after being fined £150 for 'exposing his posterior to the public view and to the annoyance of the lieges' (baring his bum) to Celtic fans during a Reserve League Cup semi-final in December 1985.

There's nothing to be worried about. We're not going to win anything, anyway.

Frank McGarvey on St Mirren's poor start to the season, August 1986. They'd failed to win any of their first six league games and had been thrashed 5–1 in the Skol Cup at Forfar. They won the Scottish Cup nine months later.

United will come to Ibrox with their World Cup men, including Negarty and Harey.

Tongue-tied Radio Clyde DJ **Richard Park**, August 1986.

Whatever happens lads, I'm proud of you for having got this far.

Dunfermline boss **Jim Leishman** in pre-match team-talk before Scottish Cup tie against Aberdeen, January 1989. It was Dunfermline's first tie of the competition.

St Mirren's team: number one, Money Campbell, eh, I mean, Campbell Money.

St Mirren's tannoy announcer gets those end-of-season blues, before the game with Dundee United, May 1990.

It spoils the whole book.

Tony Brown, author of *The Ultimate Scottish Football League Statistics Book*, January 1994, referring to one mistake (confusing Clyde with Clydebank in 1992–93 league tables) in 54,000 entries.

I SWEAR

I've never heard Matt Busby swear. He never swore.
Pat Crerand, *Only a Game?*, BBC documentary, 1985.

If some members of my kirk could hear me on a Saturday I'd be out on my ear.
Practising Christian and Airdrie boss **Bobby Watson**, November 1990.

I've been in football 30 years and swearing seems part and parcel of the game.
St Johnstone boss **Alex Totten**, answering a breach of the peace charge,
Perth Sheriff Court, 1992.

I don't swear. I like to think my command of English is such that I can disport myself in a socially acceptable manner . . . Nobody swears at the SFA. We have a young female staff here, and we don't indulge in that.
SFA chief executive **Jim Farry**, January 1994.

WAGS

You should have been where I was. I had plenty of room.
Two-goal **Bob McPhail**, after a member of the 149,547 crowd for the 1937 Scotland v England game complained of the crush.

The spot I was standing on was all right.
Rangers striker **George McLean** on being asked about the Bernabeu pitch on which Real Madrid had just beaten Rangers 6–0 in an October 1963 European Cup tie.

It was like me playing Joe Davis at snooker.
SFA selector **Tim Reid** after the 7–0 defeat by Uruguay in the 1954 World Cup.

St Peter very disappointed you didn't turn up.
Telegram sent by comic **Frank Carson** to Jock Stein after his 1975 car crash.

This is the closest I've got to Davie Cooper in five years.
Hearts defender **Brian Whittaker**, sitting next to the Rangers winger at the BBC *Sportscene* awards, December 1986.

Keeping some of the Rangers first-team squad away from a disco would be like keeping moths from a lightbulb.
Stuart Cosgrove, *Hampden Babylon: Sex and Scandal in Scottish Football*, 1991.

Such was [Joe] Beltrami's legal skills that he had already secured one postponement of [Jimmy Johnstone's assault] trial, citing Celtic's European Cup commitments as a bona fide reason. In those days Celtic were a force in European football . . . It is a legal manoeuvre that declined in currency in the '80s.
Stuart Cosgrove, *Hampden Babylon: Sex and Scandal in Scottish Football*, 1991.

It was once said, jokingly, I think, that the reason for Scotland's failure to get anywhere was that eleven Scotsmen in the same team was just too many.
Danny McGrain, *In Sunshine or in Shadow*, 1987.

If I have fallen out with Andy Roxburgh, I know the reason why. He gave me his continental adaptor in Mexico and I didn't give him it back.
Frank McAvennie, January 1987.

At the end of the day, it'll be 11.59.
Brian McClair, 1990.

More songs about Goalkeepers and Elephants.
Scotland on Sunday magazine headline in an article about Dundonian songwriter, Michael Marra, 1992.

– You bad player.
– Me bad player, but me 2–0 up.
Exchange between **Ally McCoist** and defender Luc Sonor, Scotland v France World cup tie, March 1989.

If we had rugby's 10m rule in our game, Willie Miller would have played most of his football in Norway.
Scottish Professional Footballers' Association secretary **Tony Higgins**, 1991.

We were all disappointed when Willie Miller gave up his career as a referee to go into management.
SFA Refereeing and Education Development Director, **George Cumming**, February 1994.

Andy [Murdoch] has an answerphone installed on his six-yard line and the message says: 'Sorry I'm not in just now, but if you'd like to leave the ball in the back of the net I'll get back to you as soon as I can.'
Partick captain **Jim Duffy** writing about his goalkeeper in the club programme, 1991.

He's a male nurse and the way he plays I think he's trying to get himself a few homers.
Jim Duffy on bustling team-mate Calum Campbell, April 1991.

I've got an 18-year-old's body and a 58-year-old's head.
Partick captain **Jim Duffy**, May 1992.

Every pass an adventure.
Walter Smith on cult defender Scott Nisbet, 1993.

I'm often asked how this Rangers team compares with Celtic's Lisbon Lions of '67. I have to be honest and say I think it'd be a draw, but then some of us are getting on for 60.
Ex-Celt **Bertie Auld**, 1993.

I was like a fish out of water when I was in the water.
Ally McCoist on his swimming fitness programme after a broken leg, 1993.

When I was coming here, Richard Cadette, who played along-side me at Brentford, told everyone I was Greek and owned kebab shops in London. They all knew he knew me, so they believed him. For months all the players were asking me what the kebab business was like.
Falkirk keeper **Tony Parks**, September 1993.

An enigma is a Scottish euphemism for someone who played a good game once and we're all waiting for him to do it again.
It's Only an Excuse, BBC Radio Scotland spoof documentary, 1986.

We were on a Scotland trip to Romania. As usual there had been a card school and Gordon Durie had taken a hammering. Poor 'Juke Box'. I've never seen so many losing hands. Next morning we were driving to training and passed one of those long food queues that seem a daily ritual over there. 'I wonder what they're queueing up for,' said someone. 'They're all waiting for a game of cards with "Juke Box",' I replied.
Ally McCoist, *My Story.*

I was delighted when I found out Gordon [Durie] was joining us . . . My first thoughts were 'money'. He's so lousy at cards, myself and the rest of the lads should be able to take a few quid off him on bus trips. His signing-on fee could be gone pretty quickly.
Stuart McCall on Durie's arrival, November 1993.

Which one's he?
Tongue-in-cheek reply by Alloa's **Steve Ramsay**, on being told to mark Rangers' Ally McCoist at a corner during the Scottish Cup tie between the sides, February 1994.

GIRLS, GIRLS, GIRLS

The presence of women could make speakers feel uneasy.
St Johnstone chairman **Geoff Brown**, after banning women guests from the club's centenary dinner, November 1989.

I couldn't compete with her. Andy said he wanted to stay in England and I could see why.
St Mirren manager **David Hay** after failing to entice Watford striker Andy Kennedy north, December 1991. Kennedy's girlfriend was model Maria Whittaker.

If it wasn't for Tracy [his wife], I'd be an 18-stone alcoholic bricklayer playing for Penicuik Athletic – assuming they could find a jersey to fit me.
Rangers keeper **Andy Goram**, May 1993.

If you read Nick Hornby's book [*Fever Pitch*] it's really a man's view of the game and women are a bloody nuisance at football because they don't like you spitting and swearing.
Gwen McIlroy, author of a book about Dundee United, *A View from the Ground*, August 1993.

It was almost as if two stars had accidentally collided and become one.
Jane Nottage on her January 1991 affair with Scotland coach Andy Roxburgh, September 1993.

A lot of women meeting lads that play football will think it's a great life to be in. And it is. I wouldn't run a footballer's life down. But it's a strange life. It's stranger than I imagined it to be.
Helen Rice, wife of Falkirk's Brian, *On the Line*, BBC2, February 1994.

I was talking to the wives about having other children. They said, 'Wouldn't it be nice to have another one?' I said I was fine with my two girls. One of the girls asked if I wouldn't like a wee boy. I said, 'I've already got one, his name's Brian.'
Helen Rice, February 1994.

The night before a game he will play in his sleep. He starts jumping, twitching and his arms start waving around. I've actually heard him give an interview to sports commentator Gerald Sinstadt in his sleep.

Janet Burridge, wife of Hibs' John, *On the Line*, BBC2, February 1994.

I don't think John's terribly bothered or harassed by female groupies. He isn't the prototype blue-eyed blond boy. I think if there were a few groupies that could talk goalkeeping and gloves, maybe he'd be interested.

Janet Burridge, *On the Line*, BBC2, February 1994.

FOOD

At that time [the 1880s] there was a good deal of veiled professionalism about, and Renton was called to give an account of their transactions before the SFA. It was discovered that an entry in the club books showed an expenditure of a large sum of money on chickens, and when the official, under examination, was questioned about that unusual outlay he replied blandly that the team was trained on chicken-bree, and for the rest of Renton's life it passed under the name of the 'Chicken-bree' team.
The Football Encyclopædia, 1934, on the now-defunct Renton.

Pies are probably the most sacrosanct thing in Scottish football.
Aberdeen commercial executive **David Johnson**, 1990.

A few of us want to discuss super leagues but all the rest can talk about is the price of meat pies.
Rangers chairman **David Murray** during Scottish Super League talks, 1992.

CHEERS!

In the six months that I've been at the club I haven't been in the players' bar once. It's a totally different world and it's not what I'm into at all.

Pat Nevin, *New Musical Express*, December 1983.

24 November 1913: W. Loney, who had been absent from training all week, was brought before the Board. His explanation was that he had been so upset by the big beating received the previous week that he had been very foolish and had been the worse of liquor for three days. He asked the Board for another chance.

10 March 1914: It was unanimously decided to dismiss W. Loney from the club services for intemperance and breach of training regulations and report same to SFA, Placed on open-to-transfer list.

Extract from Board minutes, Motherwell FC, quoted in **John Swinburne**, *A History of the Steelmen, 1886–1986*.

I am not a football fan. Bremner spoke to me earlier but I just ignored him. I don't know whether it was because I ignored him that he threw the drink over me.

Copenhagen barmaid **Anne Simonsen**, starting the chain of events that led to the Copenhagen Five – Billy Bremner, Joe Harper, Pat McCluskey, Willie Young and Arthur Graham – being banned for life from playing for Scotland (although Harper and Graham were both later capped), September 1975.

As recently as the late '70s, to woo our top players back home, the authorities introduced all-day drinking in Scottish pubs. It was a valiant effort that succeeded only in enticing George Best to Hibs.

It's Only an Excuse, BBC Radio spoof documentary, 1985.

It beats your tea and glucose and all the rest of it when you're looking for immediate results.

Albion Rovers chairman **Tom Fagan**, on giving players whisky before games and at half-time, February 1979.

Manager Eddie Turnbull and myself have agreed that he is available for transfer. He was told to pack his bags and get out of Edinburgh.
Hibs chairman **Tom Hart**, sacking George Best, February 1980.

Hibs had no option but to get rid of me. I've let everyone down so badly there can be no excuses. I must get away in the hope that I can lick the problem of alcohol.
George Best, February 1980.

Although I enjoyed the champagne I never let it get the better of me. I wanted to retain my faculties. I didn't want to forget.
Alex Ferguson after Aberdeen's 1983 European Cup-Winners' Cup win over Real Madrid, *A Light in the North.*

I remember Alan Gilzean telling me if I didn't drink I'd never be a footballer.
Graeme Souness, *No Half Measures*, 1985.

I won't stand for booze. One player who joined the club said, 'I may as well tell you, I like a drink.' And he did. I found out he was taking others along. You know what it's like – instead of one lager they had three. Three becomes four and it escalates. I had to get rid of him.
Teetotal Swindon boss, **Lou Macari**, 1988.

I'd sit in the pub watching the world go by thinking my life was over, drowning my sorrows. I had no trade and the only thing I could do properly had been taken away from me . . . I was at rock bottom, so I bevvied.
Ian Durrant, recalling his long recovery from knee injury, 1992.

At one of my previous clubs, the manager ordered everybody out for a drink with him. I was taking antibiotics for a stomach illness but this was not thought a good enough excuse. The evening resulted in an illness that kept me out for a fortnight.
Tranmere striker **Pat Nevin**, February 1994.

SOCIAL SIDES

We knew it was going to be quite an evening when, just before the kick-off, one of the Sporting players ran over to Willie Henderson and blurted out to him in broken English that the wee man's great pal Eusebio couldn't make it as he was playing elsewhere, but if there was anything we needed after the game, like parties, ladies, drinks, etc, it was available and the drinks were on Eusebio.

Willie Johnston, *On the Wing!*, on Rangers' match against Sporting Lisbon, November 1971.

I've always found it hard to socialise with people I was competing against. In the bar afterwards, I felt I couldn't go over to the other players . . . I wasn't unfriendly, but I wasn't overfriendly. It's only half an hour after the game, your adrenaline's still pumping. It was a bit too soon.

Graeme Souness, November 1990.

I am not the type to hang around the players' lounge with a drink after a match. The quicker I get away, the sooner I can start thinking about the game again. I'm thinking about it as soon as I get in the car to go home. I'm on auto-pilot, really.

Hibs keeper **John Burridge**, October 1991.

When I joined Celtic I weighed around 14½ stone – hardly prime condition for a winger.

Celtic's **Paul Byrne**, November 1993.

I'd never question his [Duncan Ferguson's] ability, I'd never underestimate his potential, and I'd never stand behind him in a taxi queue.

Only an Excuse '93 stage show.

Every time I have to stand in an airport beside 20 other identical shell-suits, I am acutely aware of the attitude of many fellow travellers. They whisper from the side of their mouths: 'That lot will be heading for the nearest bar, sloshed before supper, haranguing the locals, harassing the women, vomiting in the lifts and generally acting like a bunch of louts.' Actually, it is amazing how astute these observations can be.

Tranmere and Scotland winger **Pat Nevin**, February 1994.

PRIVATE LIFE

The First Post-Punk Footballer.
New Musical Express headline on Pat Nevin, December 1983.

I wanted to be an architect. What are you laughing for? I really did.
Denis Law, *Only a Game?*, BBC documentary, 1985.

I don't possess a mansion with a swimming pool, a Rolls in the garage, and a business to pay for it all. The fault is mine. The choice was mine, and knowing myself well enough – I think – there wasn't any other way.
Jim Baxter.

To suggest a player shouldn't have sex the night before a match is the height of silliness. I've had enjoyable nights and mornings before a game and it never affected me. But before a match I won't put a lot of energy into it.
Graeme Souness, 1985.

In Italy they accept going into retreat during pre-season training, they have strict codes on players' sex lives, it's almost religious. Scottish players simply don't understand that.
Graeme Souness, 1989.

The first thing I did when I got home was pick up my son Darren, who was two then, out of his cot and give him a cuddle. I discovered later the other players with families had gone home and done exactly the same thing.
Montrose striker **Ross Jack**, recalling his last game in English football – for Lincoln in the Bradford fire disaster game where 56 people died, July 1993.

He used to find it particularly funny . . . to see me using shampoo and conditioner on my hair in the bath after training or after a game. He would stand watching me and then take great pride in telling me how he had never used a drop of shampoo. If I had had a bit more courage in those days I would

have told him that was why his hair always looked such a bloody mess.
Graeme Souness on Jack Charlton, *No Half Measures*, 1985.

I've heard the workaholic thing and I resent it because it suggests a one-dimensional man and I hope I'm more than that. I just enjoy football. I have a passion for the game. That's all.
Andy Roxburgh, November 1986.

I've cried three times in my adult life. When my sons were born and when my mother died. I sometimes feel a great sense of loss and disappointment that she never saw me grow up. I left home at 15 to become a footballer, she was really proud of me; she encouraged me to go, but I know she wanted me at home. She wanted to see me grow up, it was as simple as that, but it's those simple things that are sometimes the hardest to accept.
Graeme Souness, 1989.

I would say that more than 25 per cent of football is gay. It's got to be higher than average. It's a very physical, closed world, a man's world, and you form deep bonds with people you hardly know.
Justin Fashanu of Torquay, bisexual and born-again Christian, 1992.

In football, finding religion is as bad as being gay – if not worse. John Robertson [former Nottingham Forest team-mate] started calling me Brother Justin.
Justin Fashanu, 1990.

The *News of the World* isn't the kind of newspaper I'd like in my house and I don't want to be in it.
Christian **Brian Irvine** of Aberdeen, turning down a request for an interview, 1993.

I might have had a chance of turning professional myself before getting into music. I was picked for Scotland schoolboys under-16 pool to play England, which included Billy Mackay of Rangers and Dundee United's Davie Dodds.
Skids singer **Richard Jobson**, January 1980. His brother John played for Meadowbank at the time.

Cloughie had been the one to show me the way, he was always on to me about my smoking, but it was Pete [Taylor] who kicked me up the arse at the right time. If it hadn't been for those two, I might have ended up a tramp and a boozer.
John Robertson, quoted in *His Way: The Brian Clough Story* by Patrick Murphy.

Every time I see him [then Minister for Sport, Colin Moynihan] on TV I want to put my foot through the screen.
Brian McClair, 1990.

Q: What would you do if you weren't in soccer?
A: I'd like to be a DJ.
Paul McStay, *Cut*, February 1986.

Football is like any other business. If you get wrapped up in it, you tend to think that's all there is to life. But there's so much more to life and something like music helps me to keep my feet on the ground.
Pat Nevin, *New Musical Express*, December 1983.

I don't really see myself as being a footballer all my life. When people ask me what I do for a living I don't say that I'm a professional footballer. Somehow it doesn't come out right. I usually tell them that I'm a student, which is technically true anyway. If you tell people that you're a footballer, they tend to look at you a bit differently. Some people look up to you, others look down on you, but not that many people treat you as an ordinary person, which is all you can ask really.
Pat Nevin, December 1983.

The amazing thing is that the people who put this government in power were actually the working class. Without the working-class Tory vote, Thatcher wouldn't have had a hope of getting in.
Pat Nevin, 24 December 1983.

I was a royalist when I started work as a miner at Monktonhall Colliery and I am now.
Agent **Bill McMurdo**, February 1989.

It has helped my sinus, but that wasn't the real reason. I admit it. It was 99 per cent vanity.
Graeme Souness after a 1989 nose job.

This is not a police state. Celtic want no part in secret probes into people's lives.
Celtic secretary **Chris White**, after allegations Celtic fans had hired a private detective to spy on Skol Cup final referee Jim McCluskey, October 1990.

I had been out for a night with other referee friends and fell asleep waiting for a taxi. It could happen to anyone. I am not a member of the Orange Lodge. I am quite prepared to stand up and be counted. I was not arrested during an Orange Walk. I have no prejudices.
Referee **Jim McCluskey**, 30 October 1990, on being fined £25 for being drunk and incapable, amid reports Celtic's Supporters' Association had hired a detective to investigate rumours he had been arrested for singing sectarian songs. McCluskey had refereed the Old Firm Skol Cup final of 28 October, the only controversial moment coming when he turned down an early Rangers penalty claim.

I've never been to a pop concert. I don't think I'd be missing much.
Partick Thistle boss **John Lambie**, February 1993.

Worst Moment Outside Football: I was best man at my brother's wedding when a fight broke out at the reception. I stepped in to sort it out and some bloke shoved a tumbler in my face.
Ayr's **Sam McGivern**, replying to a magazine questionnaire, March 1993.

WATSON, Michael Goodall; MP (Lab) Glasgow Central since 1989; *b.* 1 May 1949; . . . recreations: Supporting Dundee United FC.
Extract from **Who's Who**, 1993 edition.

I am lucky to have been born in the greatest time in history – the rock 'n' roll era. I spend every spare minute listening to my records.
Dundee United boss **Ivan Golac**, owner of 3,600 albums, September 1993.

I learned it [English] first of all from the songs. I knew them all. It was a relaxing time, great friendships, totally.
Ivan Golac, October 1993.

Only a Scot could be in a stookie in his wedding photos.
Leeds captain **Gary McAllister**, September 1993. McAllister broke his arm against Arsenal the day before getting married in February 1993.

You must take the counselling which you will get. It will help you grow up.
Sheriff **Charles Smith**, placing Duncan Ferguson on probation for a year for punching one Graham Boyter, September 1993.

I suppose I've become slightly disillusioned with socialism, as much as with politics itself. Something got lost along the way, there were so many opportunists. You know, a guy would stand up and say, I'm a union man, then say, I'm going to be a delegate, and before you know it, he's full-time at it, not working, and thinking he can grab power by standing up and shouting his mouth off. So much of this has made me cynical about politics in general.
   I still have my socialist instincts but, hand on heart, I veer more to the right now. A lot of people from my background are the same: you're born and brought up socialist, you earn a certain amount, and then one party says they'll tax you 80 per cent and another 40 per cent and you're left asking yourself: just how strong are my political views? Maybe that's a bit selfish, but isn't there a little selfishness in all of us?
Walter Smith, October 1993.

My taste in music is, well, catholic.
Bon Jovi and Leonard Cohen fan **Walter Smith**, October 1993.

When I finally stop playing, Allison and I might just disappear for a year. I don't know where, but after 13 years in the public eye, it would be good to merge into the background somewhere. I'll buy a motorbike and we'll do Route 66. Then we might arrive at some resort in the Rockies and learn to ski.
Ally McCoist, February 1993.

Frank gets engaged like some men have hot dinners.
Frank McAvennie's ex-fiancée **Jenny Blyth**, December 1993.

Last month on a three-day bash in Dublin with Tranmere, I was fined £20 for being a wimp and going to the cinema to see *In the Name of the Father* instead of going 'down the pub' with the lads. I shudder to think what the fine would have been had they discovered my previous day's trip to the Gallery of Modern Art.
Pat Nevin, February 1994.

There were six of us growing up in a tenement in Easterhouse. They've all got degrees except me.
Pat Nevin, February 1994.

[Film director Wim] Wenders was asked what he'd have liked to have done outside film-making. He talked about this passionate love for football. That was really memorable for me. From then on I felt a lot more comfortable mixing the cultural stuff with the football.
Pat Nevin, February 1994.

There are times when I think of referees when I'm doing one of my Keith Moon impersonations and smashing the skins.
Aberdeen's often-booked midfielder and drummer with band One God Universe, **Lee Richardson**, March 1994.

KIDS

All the directors will be jumping in their seats worrying about giving managers seven-year contracts, but, without any shadow of a doubt, it takes that length of time before you get real fruition to any sort of youth policy.
Dundee United boss Jim McLean, *Only a Game?*, BBC documentary, 1985.

You've got to entertain and to do that you've got to practise at it. And that's what's missing. The boys that I train are 16 years of age and I tell them they don't do enough here with me. If they work really hard at it, there's a possibility. But if they don't they can forget it.
Jimmy Johnstone, *Only a Game?*, BBC documentary, 1985.

My dad used to come home from work at five or six o'clock and every single day go out with me for two hours. We used to train, train, train.
Pat Nevin, February 1994.

In an international youth match here [Reykjavik] some years ago the teams were lined up and the fellow up in the booth played 'God Save the Queen'. There was a slight pause as he changed the record over to play the Icelandic national anthem, and one of our players was so nervous – I must remind you there were 10,000 people at this game and they could all speak English – one of our diplomats shouted at the top of his voice, 'Let's get into these bloody Eskimos!' For a start his geography leaves a lot to be desired and his lack of diplomacy was most embarrassing.
Andy Roxburgh, then SFA head of coaching, *Only a Game?*, BBC documentary, 1985.

My colleague with the Under-21 team, Walter Smith, told me about an incident in a Sunday League game where the boys were only ten years old, when the coach ran through the back of the goals and cleared a ball off the line to save his team losing a goal. That's the kind of hysterical behaviour you get with people who are looking after young kids in Scotland.

Andy Roxburgh, then SFA head of coaching, *Only a Game?*, BBC documentary, 1985.

To introduce children of nine and ten to football by way of 11-a-side games is just ridiculous. They should be working on basic skills rather than competing against one another.
Andy Roxburgh, July 1991.

We still approach football the way we did 100 years ago. I'll give you an example – blaes parks. The west of Scotland is the only place I've ever seen them. Whoever dreamed up crushed red shale as a suitable football surface certainly never asked anyone within the game. We had a Dutch coach over here and he couldn't believe anyone played on them.
Andy Roxburgh, July 1991.

The belief that the Brazilians have natural ability is a myth. Their ball control is so good because their kids practise and develop in the right way.
Andy Roxburgh, July 1991.

You wouldn't teach your son to swim by throwing him in the sea in the middle of winter, so why ask him to play football at that time?
Andy Roxburgh, July 1991.

You wouldn't give a child a Maserati if he wanted to drive, you'd give him a toy car.
Andy Roxburgh on SFA plans to appoint a director of children's football, December 1993.

The game here is going nowhere and the problem starts with the coaching of the kids. One day at Southampton, a coach had kids running around the ground so I asked him why he didn't give the kids the ball to train with. He said they have to be fit. At 11 or 12, they have to be fit?
Dundee United boss **Ivan Golac**, February 1994.

I thought Saudi Arabia's Under-28s played very well.
SFA official after a suspiciously mature and hirsute Saudi Arabia team beat Scotland in the final of the World Youth Championships at Hampden, June 1989.

I heard the Saudis loved Scotland because it got them away from the wives and kids.

United States Soccer Federation official after the same tournament.

THE NEW WAVE

Most players hate the fanzines. They tend to be critical of footballers and the way the game is run. Professional players are very wary of anything that makes fun of them. They can be absurdly loyal to the good image of the game.
Pat Nevin, 1988.

They said if I was unsure I needed only to look out over the Bosphorus and that would make up my mind. I told them I had recently looked out over the Clyde and that convinced me that I couldn't go through with it.
Pat Nevin on why he turned down Galatasaray of Turkey to join Tranmere, 1992.

Last Book Read: Stalin by Isaac Deutscher.
Extract from Rangers' **Neil Murray**'s questionnaire, November 1993. (Murray later noted the answer 'got me seven out of ten on the Nevin scale'.)

by contrast . . .
Best Game Seen: Any game Rangers beat Celtic.
Hobbies: Going out with lads, playing pool and women.
Favourite entertainers/singers: Female strippers.
Spotlight on **Steve Pittman**, East Fife programme, 1989.

THE FUTURE

It's ludicrous that there are so many small clubs in areas such as Fife or even in Tayside. What we were able to afford and how many people wanted to come to the game in years gone past doesn't matter. As far as I'm concerned it's only the people that want to come along now that matter. I honestly believe that clubs would be more successful if they joined and pooled resources. At the moment it's spread far too thin over the ground.

Dundee United boss **Jim McLean**, *Only a Game?*, BBC documentary, 1985.

A senior football figure in Scotland told me it [amalgamation with Dundee United] was *this* close to happening. The Football Trust was putting up £4 million for a new stadium. The city was providing the ground and Jim McLean was for it. For some reason, it fell apart then, but it will happen. I have not the slightest doubt about that.

Dundee chairman **Ron Dixon**, August 1993.

Finance is going to be sole governor of European football from now on. Television dictates sport in America and it will do so here.

Walter Smith, March 1994.

Television is a killer of 'real' football . . . global football is quite frightening, because it leaves out of account the single most important aspect of the game, namely the close personal identification most of us feel with the club we support. It is that which compels us to display our allegiance by actually going to the game, in order that we can physically join ourselves, one day every week, to the team. We go when it's not an 'event-game'. We go when it's pissing with rain and our team is crap. We go even when we know our team is going to lose. We go because we have to. We couldn't care less about Barcelona, Van Basten or Berlusconi. Frankly, mah dear, I don't give a damn who wins the European Cup. It sure as hell isn't going to be Dumbarton. If that, admittedly parochial, attitude is broken by the arrival of a European or World

League, and the next generation are only interested in televised 'event-games', then crowds for 'real' football will dwindle away. 'Our' game will be dead.

Alastair McSporran, *The Absolute Game* fanzine, April 1994.

ANON

Given this country's libel laws some of the personalities involved in the following selection must remain nameless.

Velocity.
Response by a surly member of the 1978 Scotland squad to Brazilian journalist who had asked him for 'a quick word'.

Being bollocked by Billy is a bit hard to take. It's like Dean Martin telling you to stop drinking.
Leeds player on Billy Bremner's disciplinary methods, 1980s.

Dogs are coming in off the street to play against you.
Enraged Premier League boss to off-form international defender, 1989.

I could keep a beach ball off him in a phone box.
Celtic striker discussing opponent, 1980s.

Right, I know one of you gave me a unanimous phone call last night. Who was it?
Premier League manager to players, 1991.

A coach? He couldn't coach a shite out an arsehole.
Premier League player on a member of his side's backroom staff, 1991.

INDEX

INDEX

242

INDEX